More praise for *Beyond the Glimmering Lights*

African American residents and entertainers should be recognized for the travails they endured while developing our great city. Geran has integrated the history of Las Vegas into her Aunt Mac's story, from the men who worked on the big construction projects to the entertainers who suffered the indignities of entering the back doors of casinos where they were performing as stars in the lounges. There is a rich, colorful and very moving story here — one that Trish Geran is uniquely qualified to tell.

— MAYOR OSCAR B. GOODMAN
City of Las Vegas

As an entertainer, I've benefited greatly from the trail blazed by the likes of Sammy Davis Jr., Lena Horne and Pearl Bailey — the challenges they overcame demonstrate that talent alone is not the key to longevity in Las Vegas. As *Beyond the Glimmering Lights* skillfully documents, passion and perseverance are essential traits. I am profoundly grateful for the high standards set by these amazing role models.

—WAYNE NEWTON
Entertainer, (*aka: Mr. Las Vegas*)

In 1943, only the bravest and most discontented of black Americans would leave their home for unknown territory. Trish Geran's Aunt Magnolia was one. Armed with a Bible and a handgun, Aunt Mac journeyed from her home state of Mississippi to the bright lights of Las Vegas, rumored to be a place of opportunity. What Aunt Mac found there is the subject of Geran's book, *Beyond the Glimmering Lights*. Part personal family history and part investigative journalism, Trish Geran has utilized her experience and training as a documentarian to describe both the successes and setbacks of the Vegas black community's effort to join in the glittery success of the Entertainment Capital of the World. It will surely earn a place in any complete history of the United States."

— JIM MARRS
Investigative journalist and author of *Crossfire*

Trish Geran has put a passionate, personal perspective on a story of real interest to anyone wanting to know the real Las Vegas. An important book on an important subject.

— CHARLES FLEMING
Author of *The Ivory Coast* and *After Havana*

Ms. Geran demonstrates unequivocally that in grasping the lessons of their past, people make a major advance in the struggle to determine their future. This is why philosophers have said that those who do not remember the past are doomed to repeat their mistakes.

— DR. LIGE DAILEY, JR.
Author, *History is a Weapon!*

Trish Geran takes a very personal look at a little-known segment of Las Vegas history and the foundational role played by black Americans. Part history, part self-discovery, *Beyond the Glimmering Lights*, follows the departure of a young black woman in Forties Mississippi who, in search of a better life, ultimately changes the destiny of her family and perhaps a city.

— CATELAND WHITE
What's On Magazine

Beyond the Glimmering Lights gives a panoramic view of how Sammy Davis, Jr., Josephine Baker, and others were not just entertainers — they were movers and shakers who made important contributions to the human rights movement. God knows that these activists helped put the glitter in Las Vegas.

—REVEREND AL SHARPTON
Human Rights Activist,
Founder and CEO of National Action Network (NAN)

It's important everyone know that it simply was not easy trying to make it in the city some took to calling the Mississippi of the West.

— RUTH BROWN
Entertainer, Rock & Roll Hall of Fame Inductee

BEYOND *The* GLIMMERING LIGHTS

The Pride and Perserverance of African Americans in Las Vegas

Trish Geran

Stephens Press • Las Vegas, Nevada

Editor: Geoff Schumacher
Designer: Sue Campbell

ISBN 10: 1-932173-47-1
ISBN 13: 9781-932173-475

Library of Congress Control Number 2005932563
CIP Data Available

STEPHENS PRESS, LLC
A Stephens Media Group Company

Post Office Box 1600
Las Vegas, NV 89125-1600
www.stephenspress.com

Printed in Hong Kong

Dedication

*This is the spiritual and human price
blacks in Las Vegas paid
to make what the world now calls
Sin City, U.S.A.*

Contents

One

A Reason for Leaving
The only way to get anything is to go after it.

Two

Looks Like We Made It
If I wasn't wiping mud off my shoes, I was wiping dirt.

Three

Troubled Waters
*When fear tried to move in, faith would always ease it
away.*

Four

Planting the Seeds
You never know what trouble is until it finds you.

Five

Laying a Solid Foundation
Rules were never meant for me.

Six

The Color of Money

Seven

Toast of the Town

Eight

Having Our Say

Nine

The Beginning

Ten

Last Words

Acknowledgements

The development of this book is the result of many wonderful people. I am grateful to my momma Hazel and my late father Johnus for teaching me how to be independent and that nothing comes to one that is worth having except as a result of hard work.

They supplied the seeds.

With my deepest regards, thank you Dr. Roosevelt Fitzgerald for passing the baton and insisting that I write about the place I call *my home*.

He planted the seed.

To someone I miss terribly, my Aunt Mac, the one who made me promise I would carry out this mission no matter what. Now I know what you meant.

She supplied the soil.

Dr. Lige Dailey for emphasizing the importance of black heritage to our positive self-esteem and how the omission of our contribution has negatively impacted our image and ability to dream.

He provided the water.

My dear Margaret Dalrymple, your soft and gentle yet stern words became the reservoir my inner well needed.

She restored my garden.

To my sincere and supportive friends who never stopped believing in me when many times I did and who gave me the push needed to pursue other avenues when I wanted to simply make excuses. Lee Birda, Isy, Evelyn, Yvonne, Rose, Gene, Fred, Barbara, and Cleophas, thank you for being your true selves and for the home-cooked meals.

They are my flowers.

Introduction

Beyond the Glimmering Lights, The Pride and Perserverance of African Americans in Las Vegas chronicles the struggles and victories of black residents and entertainers during the most racially unjust period in the history of Las Vegas. I tell this story through the eyes of my Aunt Magnolia Bailey, who related to me her experiences in Las Vegas from 1943 to 1960. I also pass on stories told by early settlers. In the process, I discovered that what I constantly heard while growing up in Las Vegas — that black people played a major role in the city's development — was absolutely true.

In 1943, little did Magnolia realize that a stop for a beer in a neighborhood juke joint in her hometown of Lexington, Mississippi, would change her life forever. While sitting at the bar, she met a sawmill worker named Big John who told her that he and his cousins headed to a new city called Las Vegas. After pondering for a few days, Magnolia followed her "right mind" and drove to a place she believed would afford her a decent living. With a Bible on the front seat, accompanied by a sterling silver flask of moonshine whiskey and a small handgun, Magnolia had only one more wish: to have Las Vegas in her lap and Mississippi kissing her ass.

At that time, America was in the middle of World War II, and President Franklin D. Roosevelt had announced that a magnesium plant would be built in Henderson, about 20 miles from Las Vegas. Thousands of workers were needed and the pay was $10 a day. Big John said he didn't make that in one week. He told Magnolia there also was a demand for colored women workers, mostly maid and kitchen help in white folks' homes, and the pay was just as decent.

While America was at war, Magnolia was busy making plans to pursue a better life. At the age of twenty-six, Magnolia decided to leave the treacherous Deep South for the Land of Opportunity, Las Vegas. Magnolia knew the move would be a gamble, but the idea of leaving or escaping quieted the voices of her biggest fear — having to settle for less in life.

In this book, I explore the evolution of Las Vegas' black community during the Hoover Dam era (1920s to 1930s), the Basic Magnesium plant (1940s), the rise of black entertainment (1950s) and the demise of segregation in the hotel and gaming industry (1960). I paint a picture of the time when, no matter how famous the black entertainers were, they were still treated like "just another nigger."

This is a story about how blacks came to Las Vegas with nothing and made something out of their lives; how the fight for justice and equality paid off in the end. I describe race relations in the city, unfair treatment in the workplace, indecent housing conditions and how black residents developed their own community and Strip.

In writing this book, I relied in part on the personal accounts of Magnolia, family and friends, and Magnolia's seven husbands. When it came to men, Magnolia's motto was, "When one man couldn't, another one would." The morning she left Mississippi, Magnolia was already twice divorced. Even so, she promised her mama, Leona, that she wouldn't get involved with a man until she got herself together. Then she would pick up where she had left off. In less than a week, Magnolia had a job and a rented tent, and a few months later, landed a man.

And the rest is history. . .

Chapter

A Reason For Leaving
"The only way to get it is to go after it."

At 4:30 a.m., on a clear morning in March of 1943, Aunt Mac left Lexington, Mississippi for a place she told everyone would grant her all of the things she wanted out of life. She said, "When I got behind the wheel of the car, all I wanted was Las Vegas in my lap and Mississippi kissing my ass." With a map and a Bible on the front seat, a sterling silver flask filled with whiskey peeking out the side of her half-zipped purse, Aunt Mac felt at the age of twenty six that *her* life had just begun.

To make sure the trip would be a safe one, she brought along a pearl handled handgun her second husband Bishop had given her, and placed it under the Bible. At the time it was an understood "law" that a black woman could get away with killing a black man. "They called it self-defense, but I call it 'shoot or get shot'," Aunt Mac said. As Aunt Mac drove past the cotton pickers walking on the side of the road she honked and waved goodbye with both hands.

When driving through the last little town she would see before reaching the state line, she began to reminisce about her decision to leave Mississippi and about the folks back home. The first person she recalled was her mama, Leona.

Leona was a quiet woman who spoke only when she felt it was necessary. She understood Aunt Mac, mainly because she reminded her so much of herself as a girl.

Aunt Mac was the youngest, and the most stubborn, of three kids. When she was around seven years old, she discovered that all of them had different fathers. None of the men wanted to marry Leona, and Aunt Mac was told by the family to never ask about her father. So who he was and where he lived remained a mystery.

Leona was a cook for a white family called the Stewarts. Every time she reached for that old quilted coat the Stewarts gave her many Christmases ago, or had to walk down that eight-mile, unpaved road in the freezing-cold weather, it made Aunt Mac cringe. Watching her mama, she grew bitter, and she hated the fact that she worked so hard for wages that didn't allow them to make a decent living.

Aunt Mac herself learned early about doing hard work for little pay. She began to laugh at how naïve she was the first time she picked cotton.

She loved her family and she rarely got the chance to see them, mainly because they were always working. So when her mama told her the family needed her in the cotton fields, she thought it would be a fun day in the hot sun. Boy was she wrong.

At four a.m., her mama got her up, wanting to make sure she was properly dressed for the job. On her frail body, she placed two cotton shirts and a long skirt with two slips underneath. She wrapped a cotton bandana around her head several times so the large straw hat would fit comfortably on top. She added a pair of old knit gloves with the fingertips cut out, and then she laced up her black ankle boots. Now she was ready for the fields.

Lee Birda, Aunt Mac's cousin, knocked on the door and said, "Let's go pick this cotton, girl." Aunt Mac smiled and said, "Sounds good." Lee Birda just stared at her in disbelief.

While walking toward the field, Aunt Mac realized that no one murmured a word, but then again they didn't have to. Gloom and despair were etched across their foreheads and present in their eyes. She glanced at Lee's hands and noticed how red and blistered they were, and that's when she knew this was not going to be a day of play.

"That day in the cotton field was the longest of my life. It took months for my back, and weeks for my hands to heal," said Aunt Mac. "Those darn gloves were supposed to protect my hands, but they did everything but that."

When Aunt Mac told her mama she would never pick cotton again, her mama said, "Well, it's better than nothing." This answer frustrated her and started her to think seriously about what she wanted out of life. "The first time I picked cotton for Mr. Charlie was my last time. I was ten years old and at that time I learned to be afraid. Afraid that I would have a life with no meaning and that I would have to settle for less. Since then, I was determined to make sure these fears never came true even if it would take me a lifetime."

She wanted to leave the South because she knew that if she stayed, she would end up with little or nothing in life, just like most of her relatives. The idea this might happen terrified her. As she drove past the Mississippi state line, she felt a great sense of relief. Now that she was well on her way, she began to think about her favorite pastime – men.

Aunt Mac attended Lexington Colored School of Holmes County, Mississippi, the only school available for blacks, from the first to the eighth grade. She then attended high school, which was located upstairs in the same building. Her experiences with men began in junior high.

Aunt Mac's first marriage was to a young man in Lexington named Willie Seaton. She was fifteen years old and he was eighteen. Willie was the "boy next door" who really lived next door.

Every day, Aunt Mac and Willie walked to and from school together and he insisted on carrying her books. Even after he graduated, Willie made sure he was there every morning and after her last class to escort her home. He did this until he found a full-time job.

Willie worked countless hours as a janitor at the community grocery store, which didn't allow him to spend much time with Aunt Mac. Afraid he might lose her, Willie asked her to marry him. Without any reservations, she accepted his proposal. "The reason I married Willie was to move from under my mama's feet. I wanted to make love and drink, and I knew darn well my mama wasn't going to allow it in her house."

After they were married, Willie decided they should live with his mama at least until they could save enough money to buy a house of their own. After three weeks of marriage, Willie hinted to Aunt Mac that he would like to have kids someday. Aunt Mac said, "I'll think about it, but for now, all I want is to live anywhere except next door to my mama."

Even though she didn't want kids at that particular time, she proved to be a dedicated wife. One day, the store's errand boy came over to tell her that Willie slipped and fell on a wet floor at work and injured his back. She immediately rushed to his side.

A few of her friends helped to bring him home in the car. They couldn't afford a doctor so she knew she was going to have to nurse him back to health. After a month of intensive care, Willie was on his feet and back to work.

As the months went by, Aunt Mac grew more restless about the idea of staying with Willie's mama, while he grew more content. Whenever she mentioned the idea of looking for a house, Willie turned hostile and defensive. Slowly it dawned on her: Willie was a mama's boy and there was a chance he was never going to leave his mama's side.

Aunt Mac and Willie's marriage lasted one more year. When it ended, she had no alternative but to move back home. Because she lived next door, it took only a few minutes.

The same year she divorced Willie, she married a sawmill worker named Bishop Paige. She completed two years of high school and she knew that even with a little education, she still wasn't guaranteed a decent job. So she decided to play it safe and marry a man with one. She was seventeen and he was twenty-five.

After they were married, Aunt Mac and Bishop decided to move to Jackson, Mississippi. For $2 a week they rented a small room, which was located inside a moderate-size four-bedroom house. She worked at a nearby café and he found work at the sawmill.

Two years later, things began to go wrong for the two lovebirds. Every payday, Bishop would visit the houses known to have illegal gambling going on in the back. Sometimes he would win, but mostly he would lose.

At first she didn't mind that Bishop chose to gamble after work instead of making plans with her because it gave her the chance to go out with friends to the neighborhood juke joint. She wasn't the jealous type and although she was married, she still wanted to maintain her sense of independence. "I always promised to respect my husband as long as he didn't try to boss me around. God gave me a mind to use, and it's not meant to be misused."

What she did mind was that Bishop was coming home telling bald-faced lies. He would say that he was ahead in a poker game, but then something would happen to cause him to lose his entire winnings. "Whatever his reason was, it was never his fault."

Bishop told Aunt Mac that his eye was on the big pot, and that he wanted so much to bring it home for her. Aunt Mac laughed and said, "My eye is also on the pot, and from where I'm standing it's looking awfully peaky."

Bishop continued lying, sounding more each day like a broken record. After two years, Aunt Mac decided it was over. Once again, she found herself moving back with her mama, Leona, in Lexington. "I can do bad by myself and when a fool departs from his money, I will soon depart from him."

After her divorce, Aunt Mac began to wonder: If marriage isn't the answer, then what is? She said that in those days people respected a woman if she was married to the man she was always seen with. Marriage was one of the few socially acceptable ways a woman was able to leave her parents' house if she wanted to begin a life of her own. Aunt Mac desperately wanted to prove there were other options from which a woman could choose. So, she gave herself one month to plan a strategy that would move her in another direction.

One day, while formulating her plan, in the middle of the afternoon, she decided to walk down the street to the nearby club for an ice-cold beer. Inside the club, a group of men were listening to the jukebox and shooting pool. She was the only woman in the place. She wouldn't have wanted it any other way.

Before she could sit down, one of the guys rushed over and offered her a drink. She accepted, ordering a bottle of Falstaff, and then she asked if he had a cigarette. He lit a hand-rolled white stick that he said was made with the finest tobacco in the South, then he introduced himself as Big John.

After a few rounds of drinks, Big John said, "I came to Lexington to pick up my cousin and a few of his friends. We're moving to a place called Las Vegas, Nevada, to work for a defense plant that's hiring black men and paying good money."

Big John's white boss at the sawmill in Tallulah, Louisiana, told him about the plant. He suggested it would be wise to give this new place a try.

Aunt Mac's interest was piqued when Big John told her that the pay was ten dollars a day. He said, "In all of my experiences in job seeking, I never heard of any employment paying that kind of money, especially in the state of Louisiana." He told her the potential of earning that amount practically forced him to leave the South.

Aunt Mac began to add his earnings in her head. Without counting the possibility of working overtime, she concluded that he could easily make fifty dollars a week. She laughed and asked Big John, "If you run out of ideas on what to do with all that money, let me know. I have some great ones." He said he planned to send his mama and papa money for a new roof once he got settled.

Big John had a cousin already working at the plant who said the pay was good but the living conditions were awful in Las Vegas. He also said that even though the plant was not hiring black women, there was a demand for colored women for domestic work. As long as she knew a little about cleaning and cooking, a woman could get a job in a white family's home making around six dollars a day. Aunt Mac had no problem doing that type of work. She just wanted to be paid enough to make ends meet.

That night, when Aunt Mac went home, she knew that a move to Las Vegas would be good. A few days later, she made her decision to leave, but she kept it to herself because she didn't want anyone trying to change her mind.

Big John was traveling with twelve men and they were taking only two cars. She knew it would be safer to go with them or have someone to make the trip with her, but she didn't want any company. She wanted to use this time to reflect.

Aunt Mac was surprised when her mama told her she supported her decision to leave Mississippi. She wanted more out of life for Mac and told her, "The only way to get it is to go after it."

With these words, spoken by someone she loved and respected, Aunt Mac felt she could take on the world.

After two and a half days of traveling, she finally crossed the Nevada state line. She was always confident her car would make the trip, thanks to one of her secret admirers, Engine Joe.

The day before she left, Engine Joe made sure her car was serviced and detailed. He even placed a set of new tires on the shiny, black 1939 Chevy sedan.

She wanted to look good in every way when she left. Although she didn't anticipate returning home soon, she believed in the old Southern saying, "The way you leave is the way you come back."

Looking ahead, all she could see was miles and miles of desert, but to her it represented the Promised Land. When Aunt Mac realized that in less than an hour she would be in the city she bet the folks back home would change her life and was the answer to her prayers — she made a toast, "To my new beginning. . ." And then took a long sip of the 100-proof moonshine-whiskey from her sterling silver flask and added, "and to my ending as well."

Chapter

Looks Like We Made It
"If I wasn't wiping mud off my shoes,
I was wiping dirt."

Aunt Mac arrived in Las Vegas in record-breaking time, two and a half days, because she said, "I was in a hurry to start my life." Lexington was where she was born, but Las Vegas was going to be the place she would learn how to live.

With the windows down and the cool breeze blowing through her hair, she drove down the L.A. Highway, which was one long single-lane road. When she saw a black man changing a flat tire on his car, she immediately pulled over. She walked over and introduced herself. Soon, they realized they were from the same town back home and their mamas were close acquaintances.

Aunt Mac said, "I'm supposed to be going to an area called the Westside. Do you know where that is?" The man responded, "My sister said it's west of Las Vegas. She said just keep driving down this here highway until you get to the last store on the right. Turn left and when you cross the railroad tracks just look for a bunch of black folks and heap of little old cabins."

As she began to approach a busy section of the highway (later renamed Las Vegas Boulevard and referred to as the Strip), she was surprised to find a few hotels. The two that appeared exceptional were the El Rancho and the Last Frontier.

El Rancho Hotel. Special Collections, UNLV Library

Last Frontier. Special Collections, UNLV Library

There were probably three hundred people walking up and down that one particular area. The double doors on the casinos constantly revolved as the people walked in and out of the posh hotels. After a few minutes of playing the typical tourist, cruising down the soon-to-be Las Vegas Strip, Aunt Mac suddenly realized something was missing; There wasn't a black person in sight. She couldn't help but to assume blacks weren't allowed in this part of town.

As she drove farther, she noticed a few more hotels and casinos, but they weren't as lavish as the first two. Again, she didn't see any black people and therefore drew the same conclusion.

Aunt Mac was now near downtown's Fremont Street, which was only about a mile away from the Westside. She continued until she saw the last store, turned and crossed the railroad tracks. She was now entering the Westside.

As she drove closer to where the cabins and tents were, she was shocked at how pathetic the area looked. She drove around the site to see if there was a more decent area nearby, but there wasn't. She then realized Big John's cousin was right when he described it as being awful.

Although Aunt Mac was grateful to have a chance to live in a city with a reputation for paying decent wages to black people, she couldn't help but feel a little disgusted about how depressing the Westside looked. People made homes out of cardboard, rags, and wood. The so-called houses were built close together and tumbleweeds were scattered here and there, making the area look even

1943 photo of Westside nicknamed, "Black Ghetto." Special Collections, UNLV Library

1942 photo of Westside showed little progress in one year. Special Collections, UNLV Library

more dismal. There were about two hundred black people. Some were new arrivals and some had been there for several years.

She felt the living conditions were definitely too close for comfort, to say the least, and began to feel disappointed that she had exchanged the beautiful green scenery back home for a desert. But even though it was hard to see, she still had no doubt she was in the right place at the right time.

While shopping for cold cuts and crackers at the community store, she began talking to a lady who mentioned that the hotel where she was working was hiring and to go and apply immediately.

After filling out the necessary paperwork for the position as maid, Aunt Mac was given her uniform and told to report to work the next day.

Two days in Las Vegas, and already Aunt Mac had rented a tent and found a job as a maid at a hotel on the Strip called the Last Frontier. She was earning $3.75 a day.

On her fifth day on the Westside, the residents organized an orientation of the past, present and future of the community and the blacks in Las Vegas. The informal meeting took place on a nearby patch of desert land. They felt that in order for newcomers to know where they intended to go, they needed to know where they had been.

Even though the area was not the best-looking place to wake up to, the people were friendly and went out of their way to introduce themselves. If you were a few dollars short, they took pride in loaning you the money without any strings attached — and time allowed to repay the borrowed amount was always reasonable and fair.

Aunt Mac rented a tent for five dollars a week. Her water was retrieved from a well in the backyard and the floor was made of dirt. For her bed, she used six wool blankets a neighbor had given her. With five, she made a pallet and the other one was used as a pillow.

She was proud of her place, and felt it supplied her every need. But regardless of her gratefulness, the housing for blacks was not much to write home about.

To have the opportunity to purchase land as well as a home was virtually impossible for a black person. Most of the other places in Las Vegas were off limits, and the local banks and mortgage companies refused to provide the financing to build a home on the Westside.

There was no sewage system nor were there lights on the unpaved streets. Whenever a car drove by, large clouds of dust would engulf the area, and when it rained it became one gigantic mud hole. Aunt Mac said, "If I wasn't wiping mud off my shoes, I was wiping dirt."

Driving on the roads was a nightmare. The dust was six inches or more deep and there was constantly a haze floating in the air.

Occasionally, the city would put in water hydrants and that was pretty much the only development that was occurring on the Westside, an area that rightfully justified its nickname at that time, the *black ghetto.*

The early settlers told Aunt Mac that in the late thirties a black man the town people called Old Man Mishey owned a large well and was the sole supplier of water for the residents.

Old Man Mishey would come to your "place of stay" and lay his hand-made pipes to run water from his well to your place. His pipes were made of wood and terra cotta, the pink clay used to make Spanish tiles.

At the break of dawn on the first day of each month, the residents could always rely on a visit from him. He believed in collecting his money before you left for work. Old Man Mishey was said to have had very little education but was a sharp businessman who knew how to turn a dollar into ten overnight.

Besides renting a tent, the only other option Aunt Mac had was a cabin. A man named Patrick Lisby constructed these dwellings. During his off hours from the magnesium plant and several other subsequent jobs, he would build small 12 x 12-foot cabins. The purchase price was $50 and that included materials.

After Lisby sold all his units, his co-workers recognized his efforts. They began to modify the same idea. Larger cabins, measuring 50 x 100, were built and sold for $75.

The newspapers advertised the cabins. The caption read "Cabins for Sale on the Westside." The cabins were not on solid or permanent foundations and could easily be moved from one location to another.

What Lisby and the other residents wanted most was to be able to purchase the cabin as well as the lot. They wanted to make Las Vegas their home, but the town's ordinances did not respond to their wishes.

At that time, only a few blacks owned land. They were the early settlers who came to work on the railroad in the 1920s and took full advantage of an opportunity of a lifetime.

The city was not eager to improve the Westside conditions mainly because they were convinced that once the war ended and the production of war materials was no longer necessary, the workers, both black and white, would return to where they originated.

❧ ❧

Every once in a while, the residents would brief Aunt Mac on the history of the Westside. She said originally it was called the McWilliams Townsite, which was named after a tall, red-haired Utah pioneer, John T. McWilliams.

In 1904, he was the first person to survey and plat the geographic location. He expected the area to be the new railroad town, and as a result be very profitable.

McWilliams began to sell lots to anyone who was interested. He targeted areas bounded today by Bonanza Road, Washington Avenue, and "A" and "H" streets. When the railroad tracks were completed, a tent community and a supply point were developed.

By 1905, there were 1,500 people and fewer than forty were black. The first bank, blacksmiths, wholesale houses, drug and general stores and a few good restaurants began to thrive in the young town. However, on May 15, 1905, the upswing effect began to plunge downward.

The Land and Water Company, owned by the railroad, conducted an auction to spark interest in developing an area called Clark Townsite, east of the tracks. After the auction, residents and business owners left the McWilliams Townsite, hoping to establish themselves in the new railroad town.

Disappointed by the diminishing interest in his property and plans, J. T. McWilliams decided to sell his lots at unbelievably reduced prices.

Lucretia Stevens, a friend of Aunt Mac's, bought property from him and said, "He was giving it away." Lucretia and her husband, Ernest, arrived in 1923 with four small children and came to work on the railroad.

The other ethnic groups affiliated with the railroad project were the Mexicans, Paiute Indians, and the Chinese. Despite the cultural diversity, there were no racial incidents reported and everyone who came to bid on the lots were able to do so without any restrictions.

The lots the first black families owned were located where the city decided to build its downtown. The Stevens, Shepards, Christensens and Pinstons are noted as the first to live in Las Vegas. They were from the Utah, Idaho, and Arizona areas, and were a group of very close friends.

Although there was evidence in 1905 that a few blacks lived in the area, it was never officially recorded on the city's books.

The town people called Mrs. Pinston Mammy Pinston. She owned a restaurant on Third Street between Ogden and Stewart called "The Plantation Kitchen." Her specialty was Southern-fried chicken.

The black people's homes and place of business occupied the areas between Second and Third Street. First Street was where the bordellos and saloons were located. This area was called Block 16 or the Red Light District.

Slowly, a few more blacks began to migrate to Las Vegas and reside in the downtown area. Jake Ensley was a black man from Oklahoma who was the founder of the Oklahoma Café for Negroes. Across the street from the bordellos was his restaurant, Uncle Jake's Barbeque.

Aunt Mac said the black men loved Jake's place. All day long they would sit outside, eat his mouth-watering ribs and watch the hookers parade up and down the street. Every once in a while a white policeman would catch them observing the scarcely dressed white women. He would walk up to them and yell, "Niggers, what are you looking at? Get your ass off the street."

The other black owners who arrived later were the Nettles, Levi Irving, Isaac Pulliam and J.R. Johnson. Out of the bunch, J.R. Johnson owned the largest amount of real estate downtown. Ike and Nancy Pullman leased a large section of land on Third Street that was contracted for ninety-nine years.

Ralph Simpson owned forty acres and acquired it by home-steading vegetables. The Shepards owned a café, Arthur McCants owned a barber shop, a man named Reid ran a card parlor and pool hall, and Marion Wilson operated the Gateway Hotel at Stewart and Main. Although black people managed the hotel, it catered only to whites.

The blacks who weren't business owners were more than likely ranchers, farmers, plasterers, domestic workers, porters, rail-road workers or laborers.

The bordellos were said to be off-limits to black men, but Aunt Mac said that was only during the day. She said as soon as the sun went down, a long line formed with anxiously waiting black men. They could choose only from the few black hookers who worked inside.

However, the same rule wasn't followed for white men. Nearby was a brothel that housed only black girls and the clients allowed in were white.

Lula May was a friend of Aunt Mac's who once worked at the house. She said she was just as comfortable sleeping with a white man as she was a black one. Aunt Mac said, "She was there for the money, not the honey."

❧ ❧

In the 1930s, there were 8,532 residents in the Clark Townsite. A total of 5,165 lived in Las Vegas and the remaining lived on the outskirts, which was either on a ranch or at one of the mining camps.

There were only fifty-eight blacks and they began to acquire property and build permanent dwellings. They were now considered established residents. Before, the houses were referred to as "Do Drop Inns."

Because the majority of blacks lived downtown, the McWilliams Townsite was severely undeveloped. The blacks and whites who resided in that area did not practice segregation.

Prentiss Walker was a friend of Aunt Mac's who lived downtown during the early 1930s. He said blacks could come and go in most of the business establishments except for places like the movie theaters and public swimming pools.

The two movie theaters in Clark County, the El Portal and The Palace, were located downtown and both were segregated. Blacks had to sit in the balcony or in the rows downstairs that were designated for them.

❧ ❧

Aunt Mac said the first evidence of racism the residents heard about occurred in the early 1920s. A downtown saloon called the Arizona Club was said to be, at first, a racist club. Their slogan was "Every Race Has Its Flag But The Coon." Later they changed it to "The House of Equality." Seemingly, the club could not make up its mind whether it was going to discriminate or not.

During the days of the railroad, it was common for black men to stop by the Arizona Club and other clubs near the downtown area for a bit of social interaction and libation without experiencing any problems. At first, the Arizona Club was a saloon and brothel. In 1941 it became a hotel and casino.

Regardless of the fair treatment, blacks chose to entertain themselves in their private domains. One of the popular meeting spots was the Mitchell Ranch, which became the hub of social, political and religious activity. This showed that the blacks, like the whites, continued to think in a separate but equal way, which was the lifestyle forced upon them before they arrived in Las Vegas.

Even though the white workers served the black men without showing signs of remorse, words such as "Colored Section," "Negro Quarter" and "Darky" jokes began to appear regularly in the newspapers and on signs in public places. These signs supported the fact that racism was alive and well in Las Vegas.

The following is an example of the type of humor that appeared in the newspapers:

> Two Florida darkies were watching a balloon ascension. The younger darky looked up at the big gag in amazement and then said: "I wonder what keeps that ba-loon up in the air that-a-way?"

> "Well", replied the older darky, "it is caused by various causes. Sometimes it is caused by one cause and then again, it is caused by another cause."

In 1927, the National Association for the Advancement of Colored People (NAACP) formed a branch in Las Vegas. The majority of the black residents joined and elected as their president the town's barber, Arthur McCants.

Aunt Mac lived a few houses down from Arthur. He was in his late seventies by then and he loved to sit on his porch and dip snuff. Everyone who drove by his house would honk and wave, regardless of whether he was outside or in the house. Whenever Aunt Mac had a spare moment, she would take a six-pack of beer over. Arthur loved talking about his days as the president of the NAACP Las Vegas branch and Aunt Mac loved listening.

Arthur was a tireless fighter for blacks in Las Vegas. In 1939, Arthur was furious to learn that the Race and Color Bill had been introduced in the state Legislature. He said the bill was designed to make it illegal to prevent blacks in hotels and casinos and public places. But the lawmakers were not adhering to the Fourteenth Amendment, which held that no one should be treated differently because of his or her race.

The Fourteenth Amendment was suppose to protect those who were experiencing racial bias but black Americans felt it did little to protect their rights as citizens.

Representatives from three black organizations joined forces to develop the perfect words that described how black residents felt.

The petition was addressed to the Honorable Mayor and Alderman of the City of Las Vegas, State of Nevada, in Council Assembly. It was submitted and endorsed by President Arthur McCants of the NAACP, the A. M. Brantford Club, and the Zion Mission Sunday School. It read:

> At the recent election we respectfully request this Honorable Council for an act to provide a law that all citizens or persons within the City of Las Vegas shall have full and equal enjoyment of accommodation advantages and privileges of all City property owned or leased by the City for public amusement, namely: City Parks, Golf Course, Cemetery, Swimming Pool and Library.

The petition was denied. Arthur said the dropping of the Race and Color Bill made him furious, but to refuse the petition made him damn mad. He said just as he suspected, the racial conditions continued to deteriorate, and blacks in Las Vegas did not have the numerical strength to prevent what was happening. Therefore, the blacks were forced to rely on the good will of those who did not have their best interests at heart.

Soon after, housing conditions worsened and the practice of segregation became more apparent. Black residents began to wonder how were they going to make it.

Hon. Mayor, and Aldermen of the City of Las Vegas, State of Nevada, in Council Assembly:

Gentlemen:

We, the undersigned Citizens and registered voters and tax payers of Las Vegas, State of Nevada, and supporters:

At the recent election we respectfully request this Hon. Council for an act to provide a law that all citizens or persons within the City of Las Vegas shall have full and equal enjoyment of accommodation advantages and privileges of all City property owned or leased by the City for public amusement, namely: City Parks, Golf Course, Cemetery, Swimming Pool and Library.

Respectfully submitted by

A. McCants

412 Clark Ave.
Westside.

Endorsed by the N.A.A.C.P. - A. M. Brantford, and the Zion Mission Sunday School.

1939 petition submitted by NAACP president Arthur McCants.
Special Collections, UNLV Library

Chapter

Troubled Waters
*"When fear tried to move in,
faith would always ease it away."*

Whenever negative thoughts of survival became overwhelming, the residents would practice their strong and committed belief in God. It was the only source they could rely on to keep them going. Aunt Mac said, "When fear tried to move in, faith would always ease it away."

The majority of the residents on the Westside attended church regularly on Sundays. Some even went on a daily basis. No matter how decent their salaries were or how much they went to church, it was still hard to hide the intense fears and doubts they had about their future in Las Vegas. But the truth was, they really had no better place to go.

❧◆❧

In 1905, it was said that the first church was founded. Out of necessity, the few blacks in town conducted services in their homes and called it church. Service began with the humming or singing of an old Negro spiritual. This tradition originated on the plantations. Each verse seemed to always express freedom. During slavery, when white masters would question slaves about the meaning of their songs, they were careful to explain that the freedom they were referring to would take place in the next world, not in this one.

In 1916, Reverend J. L. Collins became the pastor of the First Methodist Church. Three months later, he assisted in the organization of Zion Rest Mission Sunday School of the A. M. E. Church.

The Mission started with fourteen members. Among its officers were Mrs. L. H. Irving, the secretary, Mrs. E. J. Davis, the assistant secretary, Miss Minnie Mitchell, and the treasurer P. W. Wallace. Services were conducted at a resident's home on Thursday evenings and Bible study was held on Sunday afternoons.

Reverend Collins not only wanted to be introduced as the pastor of his church, he also wanted to be known as a minister to the people, who was always willing and ready to offer his services in any way they were needed. Reverend Collins will always be remembered as one of the most sincere men of God Las Vegas has ever had the pleasure of having.

A few years later, a Catholic priest by the name of Father Van Skee, the assistant pastor of St. Joan of Arc, initiated religious training for black children on the Westside. St. Joan of Arc was located on the other side of the tracks near downtown on the white side of town.

Classes were held at St. Joan and Father Van Skee made sure transportation was provided. Months later, he began to conduct services in black residents' homes.

In 1942, St. James Catholic Church was formed and the first priest was Father Flahize. One year later, Father Theodore Van Skee became the pastor and played a major role in reassuring the residents on the Westside that they would receive their first Catholic church.

In 1943, Mrs. Mary Nettles, one of the early black pioneers and property owners, was informed that a close acquaintance, Reverend B. T. Mayfield, was moving to Reno to start a church. Mary was not happy to hear he was relocating. She wanted him to stay. So she decided to make him an offer he couldn't refuse.

Mrs. Nettles promised to appoint B. T. Mayfield as the pastor of the church she planned to build on her property, which was located on E and Madison. Reverend Mayfield felt honored and immediately changed his mind. The church was built and named Second Baptist.

At first Mrs. Nettles wanted to start a Methodist church but the majority of the residents were from the South and were Baptist.

Mrs. Nettles created a formal agreement for B.T., which stated, in so many words, that as the pastor of Second Baptist Church, if he kept his nose clean, he wouldn't encounter any problems with her.

For two years, B.T. ministered the church successfully and was an excellent Christian example in the community. But then suddenly things took a turn for the worse.

Aunt Mac's friend Johnny was the janitor of the church. One night he walked in and just before he began sweeping, he looked up and saw Reverend Mayfield on the table making out with a woman. Johnny left before he was seen and immediately walked to Mrs. Nettles' house. He told her in detail what he had witnessed.

After the incident, Reverend B.T. became the butt of jokes for quite some time. The rumor was that he was caught putting tail feathers in an angel.

Mrs. Nettles, along with three female board members, fired Reverend Mayfield. Reverend V.C.L. Coleman was chosen as Mayfield's replacement and is on record as the first pastor of Second Baptist Church. Although the church got off to a rocky start, Aunt Mac still joined.

Practically everyone in Southern Nevada knew not to question or cause a problem with Mary Nettles. She was a tall, dark-skinned, husky woman who walked around with a .45 pistol strapped to her waist. When she signed her name she wrote S.L. Nettles, which were her husband Sam's initials.

Even the police knew to walk the other way when they saw Mary coming. One day two guys were drunk and sleeping on one of her lots. When she found out she snuck up on the guys and poured ice-cold water on their faces. Then she told them to go home and sleep it off.

Less than a block away were two policemen and they observed the entire incident. They walked over and asked Mary if she needed help. She responded, "What's the problem? Ain't nothing wrong here, just get your ass from around here. I'll handle this."

Aunt Mac said, "Mary had a clean heart but a filthy mouth, and even so, she was loved and respected by everyone."

❧ ❧

Aunt Mac's neighbor, Leddy, who was from Arkansas, came to Las Vegas to work on Hoover Dam. He said the 1930s was a pivotal decade in the history of Las Vegas. The Depression had officially started, in late October of 1929, and it literally pulled the rug out from under employment in the entire country.

In 1930, Leddy heard from a family member that there were plans to build a dam near a newly developed, wholesome town in Southern Nevada called Boulder City. This news caused an invasion of people. Suddenly, there was an average of twenty-five to thirty people coming daily. The plans were the first bit of good news since the Depression and showed promise to many who were looking for work.

Although the project was not scheduled to begin until 1931, Leddy said he and the newcomers decided to arrive early in hopes of being the first to be hired.

Homes were set up wherever they found space. Some chose to live on the Westside or near Boulder City, but Leddy said the only choice for the new blacks was the Westside. What had been a quiet little town where everyone knew each other soon became filled with strangers and these strangers brought their social morals and racial prejudices with them.

Leddy said because Southern Nevada was not prepared for this influx, the people had to make homes out of rags or whatever they could get their hands on. These areas were referred to as

Ragtowns. He thought it was a pitiful and pathetic sight, similar to the one Aunt Mac experienced the first day she arrived on the Westside.

Leddy said cars traveled in groups of five and ten. People from all over the world of every nationality came in wagons, Union Pacific boxcars, on horseback and some even walked. Leddy knew after he arrived that all he had to do was to establish a place to stay. Then his next step was surviving until the dam project began hiring.

On March 4, 1931, bids opened for the dam project. The contract was awarded to Six Companies Incorporated of San Francisco for $48,890,000, which was the largest labor contract the United States government had ever issued at that time.

On April 15th a post office in Boulder City opened and now the city was ready to provide for the dam's white workers. Blacks were not being considered.

Leddy said Boulder City was an all-white town until Al Brown, a black entrepreneur, was permitted to operate a shoe-shine stand in the recreation hall. He said Brown was not allowed to reside in Boulder City. He had to commute like the other black workers, to and from the Westside.

In 1931, while the dam was under construction, gambling in Nevada became legal. Leddy said the town celebrated because, before '31, the only games played in the state were lowball, stud, draw poker, bridge and 500.

The day after Governor Fred Balzar placed his signature on the bill legalizing gambling in Nevada, the Clark County sheriff, Joe Keate, issued the state's first gaming license to the Northern Club.

The Northern Club was located downtown. On March 20, 1931, the license was issued to Mayme V. Stocker and Joe H. Morgan. Leddy said, "Joe was a family friend and Mayme's ten percent partner."

In 1933, Prohibition was repealed with the passing of the 21st Amendment, making bootlegging no longer necessary. With gambling and the sale of alcohol legal, and the dam being hailed as the "Eighth Wonder of the World" even while under construction, Southern Nevada began to attract an array of visitors.

The hotel owners started to think about expanding or building new hotels. For the first time, definite steps toward developing the tourist trade began to be taken. There were a few small hotels downtown but there weren't nearly enough rooms to accommodate the influx.

Leddy as well as thousands of men applied for the jobs on the dam project. Some had professional backgrounds, sawmill laborers or just hard workers with a strong desire to earn a living for their family.

Leddy will never forget standing in line next to a lawyer from New York. They were applying for the same position.

The dam project required a labor force of thousands of men. The total number of workers needed for the project was about 4,000.

Even the companies transporting materials to the dam site were somewhat hesitant about having blacks on the job.

Positions were created for bringing in power lines from Southern California, building a roadway from Las Vegas to the site, constructing a railroad spur and building Boulder City. Hundreds of men were needed to complete these projects but only a few blacks were hired.

Leddy and the other black men did not find out they were not going to be hired until after they arrived. Some decided to leave and some waited. Leddy heard that the reason they were turned away was because they had to be "bona fide" citizens of Nevada and have experience working on a dam. Jesse, a white man who was a friend of Aunt Mac's fourth husband, Lancey Williams, said, "They knew damn well no one had any of that."

In 1931, Jesse moved from Missouri. He came to work on the dam project. On the day he went to apply, they issued him a uniform, hard-hat and boots and immediately put him to work. No one asked if he had any experience or if he was a permanent resident.

The black men had to wait almost two years before they were hired. In July of 1932, the first ten blacks were hired and the pay was fifty cents an hour.

Throughout their stay on the dam site, Leddy said they were not well received by the company or by the white workers. Not only were the work conditions uncomfortable, so were the living conditions.

Leddy said he will never forget when the *Las Vegas Age* newspaper ran a discriminating editorial that described both the project and its employees. The black workers who played a major role in the construction of the miraculous project were furious. The article read:

> When Boulder Dam is completed, it would have been an average number of nearly 4,000 employees who rolled up the stupendous number of 71,500,000 mandays worked, by the typical dam worker of 37 years of age, white, American born, representing every state in the union.

In 1936, the contractors completed the dam project in five years – exactly two years, one month, and twenty-eight days ahead of schedule. It was reported that upon completion of the dam, 42,000 people applied or wrote letters of inquiry.

The dam was called Hoover Dam, named for the president of the United States at the time it was started, Herbert Hoover.

When President Franklin Delano Roosevelt was sworn into office, the dam was still under construction. On September 30, 1935, Roosevelt dedicated the dam as a "twentieth century marvel" and decided to rename it after the nearby city, Boulder.

1931 Hoover Dam construction workers. Special Collections, UNLV Library

But in 1947, President Harry Truman suggested the original name be restored. An act of Congress was passed and the name was once again Hoover Dam.

When the excitement of the dam's construction was over, in 1936, the population of Boulder City dwindled but remained all white. Aunt Mac said, "The town wanted to maintain their wholesome image even though they knew the residents came to Las Vegas to cut loose and let their hair down."

The majority of the white work force went back to the South and northwest for other projects they heard were under way. When the boom period was over, another sign of segregation awakened in Nevada.

Aunt Mac's third husband, Leroy Jefferson, and his friend Ottis experienced a great deal of harsh treatment after the dam was completed. There were only a few blacks who decided to stay and Ottis and Leroy were two of them.

Magnolia and Leroy, her third husband. Geran Family Collection

With the exception of the blacks who were fortunate enough to find employment with local businesses or become contractors on small projects, those who had no visible means of support were told by the constables to move on.

Vagrancy laws began to go into effect. With the fear of becoming imprisoned, many black men decided to leave, which is what Ottis should have done.

On a scorching, hot afternoon, Ottis was fresh out of cigarettes. He decided to take a chance and walk to the neighborhood store. Suddenly, a truck pulled up behind him carrying three white men. A voice yelled out, "Lay on the ground, boy!" Ottis was worn down and he didn't want any trouble, so he gave in and laid across the hot pavement.

He raised his hands in the air and freely admitted he was not working and that lately, bad luck had been his closest friend. Not wanting to hear any of his excuses, the constables handcuffed him and threw him in the back of their dirty, old, blood-stained truck. Apparently the truck was used to transport slaughtered pigs.

Ottis was jailed and sentenced to work on a chain gang for six months. Aunt Mac said, "You never know what trouble is until it finds you."

The vagrancy law allowed the constables to make the choice of three punishable acts. The prisoners had to either sweep the unpaved streets, dig ditches for the sewer system or were placed on a chain gang. The constables decided the length of the sentence.

The unemployed black men felt that if they wanted to be treated like a bunch of animals, they should just go back home. At least they would have the comfort of being around their families if something bad happened.

The black men knew that this suddenly created vagrancy law had them in mind before and after it was enforced. The newcomers were kept pretty much on the run. Only a few managed to remain and become part of the town.

The first serious forms of racism were the hiring practice on the dam project and then the vagrancy law. Still, Aunt Mac said, "In the early years of Las Vegas' history, blacks experienced very little racial problems compared to the number of incidents that were reported in the Deep South."

By 1940, the total population in Las Vegas was 8,422, and only 178 of those residents were black.

4
Chapter

Planting the Seeds
"The hookers could stay but the black folks had to go."

After the completion of the dam, 250,000 to 365,000 people were visiting Southern Nevada on a yearly basis. Entrepreneurs began to recognize Las Vegas' potential and the first form of action toward development was to rezone the downtown area.

Businesses that did not cater to tourists were driven out. They were asked to leave and if they refused to do so, their license would not be renewed. Among those who were asked to relocate were the few black owners. Although every case was supposedly questioned and advised accordingly, they were actually being pushed out.

Fremont Street was changing, and the plans and the vision for its future did not include blacks, especially those in ownership positions.

The bordellos, however, were considered to be businesses that catered to the "new trade." Aunt Mac said, "The hookers could stay but the colored folks had to go."

The Westside continued to remain largely undeveloped. It remained a pitiful and pathetic sight.

The whites who lived there were not particularly happy about the prospects of more colored people moving in. In fact, they hated it so much they formed an organization called the Westside Improvement Association.

On February 1, 1940, the association submitted an ordinance to Mayor Russell and the city commissioners asking that the Westside be segregated. R.L. Christensen, president of the Las Vegas Colored Progressive Club and the corresponding secretary, H.L. Wilson, responded to the petition.

Christensen and Wilson asked that the city not segregate a portion of the Westside for caucasians only. They also stated: "We are true American citizens who have fought and died for our country and yet you will find lots of people living in this section (as identified in this petition) who are foreigners and have never done anything to establish American independence."

R.L. Christensen, as well as the black residents, knew if the segregation law passed, the next request would be for them to leave the city.

The city really had no choice in the matter. They either had to allow the black businesses to remain downtown or rule against the Improvement Association's petition. The commissioners opted for the later, which caused the majority of the whites to relocate. Aunt Mac said, "White folks had plenty of other options. The least they could do was to allow us the opportunity to have our one."

The McWilliams Townsite, now known as the Westside, was being transformed into a black community with new businesses owned by their own kind.

As more and more blacks were directed or drawn to the Westside, businesses that serviced the needs of the residents began to appear. Barber and beauty shops, bars, soda fountains, neighborhood stores and cafes were established.

However, the majority of blacks, especially the old-timers, felt there might be a negative side to having these new developments while there were still several whites and a few Hispanics living there.

They suspected that as long as non-blacks remained on their side, there would always be voices of opposition and resistance to their desire to become treated equally. They also feared that the more the Westside provided for the residents, the easier it was go-

1939 letter written by R.J. Christensen asking the mayor to not segregate the Westside. Special Collections, UNLV Library

ing to be for the city to enforce more off-limit areas. What they wanted was continued access to the downtown areas.

Hotels, casinos, and entertainment were still in an embryonic stage but the number of visitors a day began to triple and the city was forced to place tourism at the top of the list.

A metamorphosis was about to occur and segregation would sooner or later take place.

A memorable moment for Aunt Mac was the day she heard that Germany had invaded Poland. It was in September 1939 and the attack caused World War II to be initiated. She was walking to the corner store back home when suddenly a man yelled, "A war has started!" Two days later, President Roosevelt declared that the United States would remain neutral and Congress strongly supported his declaration. Everywhere she went, a radio was blasting the latest news on the war.

Under the Neutrality Act of 1937, the president reluctantly prohibited the export of arms and ammunitions to any of the belligerents. On September 8th, following the proclamation of a limited national emergency, Roosevelt urged Congress to repeal the arms embargo. On November 4th, the Neutrality Act of 1939 was passed and the president got his wish.

Roosevelt's repeal of the embargo had a tremendous effect on the economic well-being of the United States. Factories and defense plants that had closed with the onset of the Depression reopened throughout the country to manufacture war materials needed by the allies.

The opening of the plants made it possible for close to a million people who had been unemployed during the course of the Depression to be able to earn a living again. Aunt Mac said that while America was back to work, black people were busy fighting for justice in the workplace.

Seventeen months after the repeal, on June 25, 1941, the president issued Executive Order 8802 stating that discrimination in defense or government jobs would not be tolerated. This ruling can be greatly attributed to the tireless effort of A. (Asa) Philip Randolph and others who spearheaded the cause.

Under the leadership of Randolph, protests were lodged and a massive march was threatened to take place on July 1, 1941, in Washington, D.C., if changes did not occur.

Aunt Mac said, "A. Philip Randolph was a handsome black man who was a porter for the Pullman Company, which was one of the most powerful business organizations in the country." The Pullman train porters chose Randolph to head their unionization efforts because they trusted him, and because he was a good orator and a fighter for civil rights.

In 1925, Randolph organized the Brotherhood of Sleeping Car Porters. From that position of power he was influential in the formation of the Fair Employment Practices Committee (FEPC). At one time, A. Philip Randolph was labeled as being the most dangerous Negro in America.

Another memorable day for Mac was when Roosevelt put an end to unjust and unfair treatment at job sites all over the world because of the request by a black leader.

Executive Order 8820 stated in part:

> There shall be no discrimination in the employment
> of workers in defense industries or government because
> of race, color, creed or national origin.

Before the Executive Order was issued, Congressman Scrugham of Nevada was interested in establishing a magnesium plant in the state. He conveyed his desire to the secretary of the Interior, Harold L. Ickes, and Ickes, in turn, made the plant interest known to the president.

The Basic Refractories Company of Cleveland, Ohio, had mining claims on large deposits of magnasite and burcite at Gabbs, Nevada. Once the technology had been discovered, they took the necessary steps for mining and refining those raw materials. Two plants were needed, one at the mining site and one for processing. The latter was built in Southern Nevada and the town that grew up around it was at first called, Basic Townsite, but later was named Henderson. The plant was located on 2,800 acres of desert roughly halfway between Las Vegas and Hoover Dam.

Less than one month after the Executive Order was passed, the Defense Plant Corporation authorized that the construction of the Basic Magnesium plant be located in Southern Nevada.

World War II was under way and although the United States was not actively involved in the fighting, it became what some called the "Arsenal of Freedom."

On December 7, 1941, at 7:55 a.m., the United States suffered its first sneak attack. While America was busy paying close attention to how Germany, under the dictatorship of Adolph Hitler, was bombing the "Mother Country," England, Japan bombed Pearl Harbor in Hawaii. It was the first time in U.S. history that an attack had been made on American soil.

Japan wanted to acquire the rich resources of Asia but the United States protested against it. The U.S. demanded that Japan stop its actions but the request was ignored. Japan had only a few natural resources and relied heavily on U.S. exports.

When Japan continued its aggressive efforts to expand throughout Asia, the United States decided to cut off exports of petroleum and other goods indefinitely. The Japanese felt the U.S. was blocking its efforts and therefore decided to cripple the U.S. Pacific Fleet.

Japan had thirty-three ships that launched 350 airplanes against the U.S. Fleet. The chief targets were eight battleships among the 180 American vessels anchored in the harbor. The attack killed 2,388, wounded about 2,000 and destroyed twenty-one American ships and more than 300 planes. Aunt Mac said, "They wiped us out and now it was time to take the clutch out of neutral and move into overdrive."

On December 8th, Roosevelt addressed Congress. He called December 7th "a date which will live in infamy." On that same day, Congress declared war on Japan. Roosevelt urged Americans to back the war effort and avenge Pearl Harbor. He said, "Every single man, woman and child is a partner in the most tremendous undertaking of our American history."

In July of '42, about 100 people a day came to Southern Nevada hoping to work at the magnesium plant. Out of all of the summer months in Las Vegas, July was the most miserable. Aunt Mac left the South for Las Vegas in March, because she heard the weather would be cool and breezy and that it would make the trip more pleasant.

There was a demand for 13,000 workers. This required amount would now cause Henderson to surpass Las Vegas' population, which was 8,422, making it the second largest city in the state.

Aunt Mac's neighbor Leddy managed to find work and make Las Vegas his home. When the plant opened, 4,000 people came looking for work.

Leddy said the Basic Magnesium plant at first did not want to hire blacks. In fact, they were turned away at the door and were not given an explanation. In the South, many of the men were told that blacks were being considered for hire, but when they arrived they were told just the opposite. As the revitalized economy made gains and white Americans were forging ahead, blacks were falling further behind.

By being born and raised in the South, blacks simply became accustomed to all sorts of segregation. It was no secret that their economic conditions were the worst in the entire country.

Aunt Mac said, "Traditionally, blacks were the last hired and the first fired, and the victims of job discrimination in the United States." In other words, blacks were already involved in their own Depression long before the stock market crash in 1929.

Fortunately, the door stayed closed only for a short time. A few months after the plant began its construction, blacks were hired, and Leddy was one of them. The pay was eight dollars a day. Although they were earning decent wages, the living conditions began to worsen. Trying to secure decent housing was now the biggest challenge.

1941 Basic Magnesium Plant – no blacks in photo. Special Collections, UNLV Library

Six months later, blacks were present at Basic Magnesium Plant. Special Collections, UNLV Library

When the newcomers arrived in town, they discovered that one of the issues they tried to escape from back home was what they had traveled to: homelessness. They had no idea that their car or a lawn would be the place they would call home for a while.

There were an inadequate number of places available and those areas were segregated. Basic Magnesium provided only 324 places for blacks to reside. Those accommodations consisted of 64 dormitories with no bedroom, 104 one-bedrooms, 104 two-bedrooms, and 52 three-bedrooms. These rooms provided for fewer than two-thirds of the black workers.

A contract was granted to the McNeil Construction Company to build housing for the workers, but it included a clause stating that the dwellings should be designed as temporary and demountable. The local officials were convinced that when the war ended, the workers would return home. Aunt Mac believed that this clause was written with black folks in mind.

The Hammes-Euclemiler Company of Los Angeles constructed living quarters for blacks near the plant for fewer than a thousand. Based upon the influx of men who were moving to that area, it was not nearly enough.

The blacks were relegated to an area near the plant called Carver Park. Their other choice was to commute from the Westside. Carver Park was named after George Washington Carver, who was known as the Peanut Man. His research to develop commercial applications for peanuts was the greatest of all his accomplishments. Black people looked upon him as an inspirational leader who rose above unfair conditions and proved that a black man could be the intellectual equal of a white man.

These two handpicked areas for blacks were not comparable to where the whites lived. In fact, the living conditions of the houses were totally opposite.

Also in that letter to Big John, his cousin said there were no rooms available where he stayed, so when he arrived he might have to sleep in his car, on the lawn at the post office or at the courthouse.

Big John's cousin rented a room in a G.I. hospital tent for $7 a week. This included room and board and two meals a day and the tent was located in Carver Park. A man from Phoenix, Arizona, named Ray Lucas owned the tent. The tent was approximately 40 feet long and 14 feet wide. There was no heat in the winter and no air conditioning in the summer.

There were no medicine cabinets, just orange crates set beside cots with a sack underneath. Because many of the men knew each other from back home or were family members, they felt safe enough to lay their wallets and watches underneath the bed when they retired for the evening and the lights were turned out.

The struggles and conditions that existed back home generated a genuine concern for one another. That knowledge and kinship allowed them to live in such close quarters. Surviving this terrible ordeal was the common thread that held them together. Soon after, Ray Lucas transformed a house trailer into a café for his tenants.

Carver Park had a special school for black children. Not much was reported about its activities except that the teachers viewed them in a stereotypical manner. An article in the *Las Vegas Age* quoted a teacher who said, "All of the children have good voices and all have an uncanny sense of rhythm."

Carver's segregated school was different in only one respect from the schools in the South: The teachers were white.

One of the reasons why the parents of the kids did not object to segregation in the school was because they were familiar with the realities of it in the South. Most of them had little education and they simply wanted more for their children.

The white workers lived in an area near the plant called Victory Village. A trailer park east of Victory Village was also built that had electricity, water, showers, laundries and access to toilets. It was said to be one of the best in the United States.

The other choice was a newly constructed subdivision east of Las Vegas called Huntridge. The Huntridge Development Company announced that in mid-December modern two-bedroom dwellings and duplexes would be available to Basic Magnesium employees and their families. They were for rent or for purchase with a thirty-month option to buy.

A month later, the O.J. Scherer Company announced 300 apartment-type dwelling units to go up east of the main highway and south of Anderson's camp. They would be one-, two- and three-bedroom apartments with living room, kitchen and bath. These spacious community houses included an assembly hall and play rooms. However, the newly developed units were never intended to ease the dwelling crunch of the black workers and their families.

The lack of housing for blacks caused hundreds of makeshift shelters to be built. These put-together shelters were crude and had no facilities.

The Westside was still in its formative stage and therefore was not prepared for the influx of people. However, as hundreds of black people moved into the area, the whites and non-blacks moved out.

The Basic plant had three shifts and the production far exceeded expectations. Once the United States entered World War II the country was prepared. Aunt Mac said, "Everybody was willing, able and ready."

The men at the plant were paid an average of $1 an hour. Sometimes a normal forty-hour work week with eight hours overtime at a rate of time-and-a-half resulted in take-home pay of $53. To be able to make enough money to survive on, to save for a rainy day and then send a few extra dollars back home was a dream come true for blacks.

Because of a lack of housing, the migration of blacks to Las Vegas, and the commuting to and from the Westside to Henderson helped to fuel the fires of racism.

In one decade, from Hoover Dam (1931) to the Basic Magnesium plant (1941), Las Vegas was transformed from somewhat of an integrated community to a segregated one.

જાજી

Reverend Bill Stevens, president of the local branch of the NAACP at the time, began to raise the awareness of blacks. He enabled them to see that they had self-worth and dignity in ways they have never seen before.

Aunt Mac said Reverend Stevens was known for his peaceful lunch counter sit-in protest. She said that every day of the week he would take a newspaper and a book and head for the downtown restaurants. Because he was black, he knew he was not going to be served.

Reverend Stevens said he enjoyed sitting back, reading and wondering what made him so different. When a white customer came into the restaurant and sat next to him and said something like "It's a nice day, isn't it?" Stevens would reply, "Certainly is, especially if they would serve me a cup of coffee or a cup of tea."

The black workers at the Basic Magnesium Plant believed that his continued protest caused them to clearly see that the unfair treatment at the plant did not have to be endured. It wasn't going to be business as usual. Not only were the housing accommodations humiliating, so were the working conditions.

After six months of operation, the plant managers discovered that the heat in the plant was unbearable to many of the white workers. Suddenly a demand to hire more black men to fill these positions was requested.

Even though the majority of the black workers were from the South, they had not been exposed to the set of circumstances that were happening at the plant. The stereotypical view of them was not a major concern. What bothered them most was the extent of segregation in the workplace.

Aunt Mac's second boyfriend in Las Vegas, Ernest Humes, worked at the plant and said there were segregated crews, water fountains and areas in the cafeteria. Aunt Mac said, "The pay was great but the treatment and work conditions was so darn harsh on the guys."

One day, after the end of the day shift, 200 black workers staged a walk-out protest. A representative from the Fair Employment Practices Commission came to investigate. After thoroughly researching the safety and working ethics that were being practiced, he understood the reason for the protest. He recommended that these segregated practices be stopped immediately.

Conditions at the plant began to improve in various ways. Ernest's friend was promoted from a senior clerk in personnel to a foreman in one of the plant's labor divisions and the in-house publication began to feature photos and short articles about blacks on the job, on the Westside and at Carver Park.

Topics discussed in the publication included black children at the Carver Park School, the birth of twins by a worker's wife and Jack Johnson, who in 1910 officially became the first black heavyweight boxing champion after beating the "Great White Hope," Jim Jeffries.

The workers noticed there were no visible signs of integration in the photos. They then concluded they were involved in their own war that was occurring inside the walls of the plant.

Aunt Mac said, "The war did not do much to eliminate segregation. In fact, it was a major contributor."

World War II had necessitated the establishment of military camps in nearby areas like Southern California, Arizona and within the state of Nevada. When the soldiers received their weekend passes, the majority would visit Las Vegas.

The numerous military bases were all segregated. After the soldiers arrived, they soon discovered Las Vegas was, as well.

The downtown saloons and the two hotel-casinos on the Strip were off-limits to black soldiers. The policy of no coloreds made it apparent that there was a need on the Westside to construct places such as these.

Temporary housing for black soldiers was very much needed. Knowing this, the black residents decided to open their homes, inadequate as they were. They continued to do so even after the black United Services Organization (USO) began to use the recreation hall for housing and activities.

The recreation hall was located at the corner of D and Jefferson on the Westside.

For Thanksgiving, the residents were asked to invite the soldiers over for dinner. Most of them could not afford to go home for the holiday. Feeling honored and blessed that she was able to provide a meal for someone, Aunt Mac decided to invite four soldiers.

Slaving half the day over a wood-burning hot stove, she prepared a five-course meal. The table setting was so beautiful the soldiers wished they had a camera so they could send a picture home.

Two of the guys were from the South and the other two were from Arizona. They were in their early twenties. Aunt Mac asked about their women or wives back home and she wanted to know when was the last time they wrote their mothers. At one time, they each pulled out their wallets and showed her a picture of their mama. That's when she knew she was among gentlemen.

When dinner was ready, she carefully placed the mouth-watering dishes in the middle of the table. When she sat down, the handsome soldiers proceeded to do so as well. They then thanked her for being so hospitable and for going out of her way for them.

She suggested they hold hands while she said grace. As soon as everyone said "Amen," suddenly a strong wind came and blew the entire tent down. The table tipped over and the food fell on the floor. Every morsel was saturated with dirt. The food that took all day to cook was ruined.

Aunt Mac was shocked and mad as hell as she stared in total disbelief at the food on the floor. She hardly recognized the turkey, the green beans, the macaroni and cheese, the yams and the hot buttered monkey bread that had taken so long to prepare.

The officers consoled her and said it was the thought that counted. Aunt Mac quickly responded, "Thought, hell, it ain't every day I cook. I feel like I had worked all day in the cotton fields and after I turned in my bag Mr. Charlie walks away without giving me a penny. That's as low as you go."

Suddenly, she remembered that around the corner was Roy Rillar's Cafe. He was open, but he was only serving hot dogs and hamburgers. The soldiers didn't care. They were so hungry they seriously considered washing the dirt off the scrumptious-looking food, and acting as though nothing ever happened. Aunt Mac knew they were soldiers and they were taught how to survive on little or nothing, but she refused to hear this plan.

⅋⁊

The Basic Magnesium plant was ahead of schedule. In 1938, only 2,400 tons of magnesium was produced in the United States. In 1943, more than one hundred times this amount was available.

By November of 1944, the government did not need any more magnesium. Production was stopped and the large plant became idle, causing the majority of the workers to be laid off. A concentration camp set up for the Japanese citizens remained open.

The camp was located near the railroad tracks at A and Owens on the Westside. The residents didn't refer to it as a camp. They felt that because there were only a few Japanese in town, it really was more like a farm. They were more comfortable calling it Jap Farm.

Most of the workers who left Southern Nevada were white. The black workers had already sent for their families so they saw no reason to leave, not just yet.

Even with the segregated rules and policies that were becoming a way of life for blacks, Las Vegas still showed more promise than the South. At least they were allowed to vote. In the South they were still denied this right.

Black women were starting to earn as much as $6 a day doing domestic work in private homes. The newspapers were filled with job announcements soliciting help from colored women.

Black women not only found work in the homes, they also began working as maids and kitchen helpers in the developing hotel and gaming industry. The black men who were laid off at the plant were able to find jobs as porters, groundskeepers and janitors at the hotels.

Blacks began to build simple dwellings on the Westside. They now considered it to be their home. The Basic Magnesium plant had an enormous impact on the black population.

In 1945, World War II was declared over. Now the city could begin its plans to become a tourist mecca.

Chapter

Laying a Solid Foundation
"Rules were never meant for me."

The 1940s marked the beginning of the hotel, casino and entertainment era in Las Vegas. Practically every week a new hotel was breaking ground along Fremont Street and on the Strip.

As the business on Fremont Street increased, the presence of the bordellos on First Street was no longer required, and they were asked to leave.

In the state at that time, prostitution was not really outlawed. However, what would make it a misdemeanor is if it was discovered within 400 yards of a school, church or public facility.

Prostitution is the world's oldest profession and the world's oldest business is gambling.

Now that the tourists were both men and women, Aunt Mac said the bordellos were becoming a little distasteful. The wives began to accompany their husbands to Las Vegas and it just wasn't professional to have the hookers parading in front of them.

During the war, the bordellos were asked to leave because the black soldiers started to get pushy with the black girls. Because there were so few registered with the houses, the soldiers literally began to fight over them. These outbursts became frequent and the surrounding establishments and their clientele were being affected. The city felt that even though it would be easier for the bordellos to leave downtown, the timing was not quite right.

A private, gated small business complex was developed called Formyle. It was located exactly four miles from Las Vegas on Boulder Highway. A bar, laundromat and brothel called Roxie's Resort was located on the compound. It was said that most of the hookers from First Street went to work at Roxie's. The owners were Roxie and Eddie Clippinger.

The Clark County sheriff at that time, Glen Jones, made sure the brothel operated without any interruptions. He had special interests in the place and one was receiving generous payoffs for favors and cover-ups.

Trying to gain entrance into Formyle without the proper verification was virtually impossible. When you drove in, the first thing you saw was a guard shack. A security guard was present twenty-four hours a day.

The guard would then check to see if your name was on the list. If it wasn't, you were told to immediately turn around and exit the premises.

Roxie's Resort was once called the "best and most fabulous little whore house in the history of Las Vegas."

Aunt Mac was offered a better-paying job as a servant at the Las Vegas Army Air Field in the Officers Mess Hall. She was earning $5 a day, which was a little more than the $3.75 she was making as a maid. She said, "Every little bit counts."

She loved working around all those men at the air base and apparently the feeling was mutual. They thought she was a pretty black woman. they thought she resembled Lena Horne so much that they gave her the nickname Little Lena.

Aunt Mac was a very attractive and proud woman with long, silky black hair, accompanied by long, silky legs. She enjoyed expressing her soft, feminine charm, slinging her hair back and forth every chance she got. She knew it was considered taboo for a black woman to sling her hair like a white girl, but like she always said, "Rules were never meant for me." Men flocked to her wherever she went. They loved her and she loved them and to her that was a great combination.

"The one thing the guys in the Mess Hall knew how to do was drink without getting drunk," she said. The officers were very clever about how and when to consume alcohol. They would bring their own bottles and when they were finished pouring, they would make a mark that showed how much was left. Even if was just a "corner," they marked it. To them, a little was still enough to come back to.

Keeping track by marking their bottles was the best way the officers knew how much they had just consumed in one sitting. On their way out of the club, they would walk, or sneak, if it was in the middle of the day, behind the bar to place the little glass containers on the bottom of the shelf. Then they would give it a push until it was no longer visible to the naked eye.

Magnolia's Las Vegas Army Air Field officer's mess hall work badge in 1946. Geran Family Collection

When the officers left the hall, Aunt Mac would clear and clean the tables. Just to be on the safe side, she would look behind the bar to make sure everyone had placed their bottles accordingly.

A few years before Aunt Mac started working at the air base, the entertainer Pearl Bailey had performed on the base. In Pearl's autobiography, *The Raw Pearl,* she described her first experience in Las Vegas:

In 1941, during the war, we played at a base in a place called Las Vegas. When you got off the train, there was Main Street and inside all those places people were throwing dice and playing slot machines, with police-men looking on. None of us had seen anything like it before and, at that time, other than people who'd been abroad to Monte Carlo, other folks in America hadn't seen it either. We went into those spots and played the machines.

With her first paycheck from the air base, Aunt Mac decided to rent a room at Brother Powell's spacious three-bedroom house, located at G and Monroe on the Westside, for $4 a week. The Las Vegas Army Air Field was later renamed Nellis Air Force Base.

It was common for Aunt Mac to have two or three jobs. She believed in having her own money. One of her favorite lines was "God bless the child that's got her own." Aunt Mac always had a knack for finding work in the most unusual places. Sometimes her personality would contradict where she worked.

One day, Lula May, her friend and ex-prostitute, suddenly became ill. She had "female problems." She asked Aunt Mac if she would fill in a few weeks for her at her place of business, the Chicken Ranch bordello. Without hesitating, Aunt Mac saw no problem in stopping by the brothel on her way home. It was near the air field, so it wasn't an inconvenience. Lula May was a seam-stress and maid at the Chicken Ranch.

The first time Aunt Mac walked into the large, white house, there were about fifteen white girls parading around in slinky lingerie. Aunt Mac pretended she wasn't surprised at the unusual setting. She immediately grabbed the "costumes" that needed mending. She began to alter the ripped material, replace the miss-ing buttons and repair the torn zippers.

The customers were all white, mostly soldiers, and the doors were open twenty-four hours a day. Sometimes the guys would take hours before choosing the girl they wanted to be with. By talking to the girls and observing how they mingled with their customers in the waiting room, the men were able to make up their minds.

The madam was a heavy-set white woman with large, double D breasts and she was aware of everything that went on inside those walls. She was the one you made your request to and the one you paid.

One time, she suspected a customer of taking longer than what he paid for. She ran up the stairs, knocked on the door, and said, "Excuse me, has there been a change in plans?"

Aunt Mac liked being around the girls. They would tell her their problems as though they had known her all their lives. She looked at them as friends and deep down she kind of felt sorry for them. She said they acted like little lost sheep.

After four weeks of recuperating at home, Lula May was ready to come back to work. Aunt Mac used the extra money she earned wisely: She decorated her room and sent money to her mama.

❧ ❧

The Las Vegas Water District was now supplying the Westside's water and Clark County finally developed a sewage system. The city even sent a truck by twice a day to hose down the dusty roads. The only paved area on the street was the bus route.

Because the Westside was considered a small community, the white mail carrier was able to deliver the mail twice a day. It was also a great way for him to justify his eight hours. With these developments, blacks were now able to build stable, permanent houses and own more businesses, in addition to the ones that had been relocated from downtown.

Roy Christensen was a janitor at a movie theater downtown. After it was torn down, he transported the bricks to the Westside. He built a beautiful two-story house that enhanced the area tremendously.

Harvey "Daddy" Jones was one of the few apartment builders and owners in town.

Side Burn Johnson, on the other hand, had been building homes for people since the 1930s. His homes were known to lean a little. Aunt Mac said, "You would think that the more homes a person built, the better he would become at it."

The community began to gain access to an array of businesses that catered to their needs. For example, instead of having one store to shop at, now there were quite a few to choose from.

Rollin Johnson and Harvey "Daddy" Jones opened a grocery store, One-Arm Wingy Hughes opened a grocery and a liquor store and Jim Tatum opened Tatum's Barbeque. The other establishments were beauty parlors, barber shops and a cleaners. A few more churches were built as well.

The Westside was getting a face-lift and was becoming a "town within a town." The residents felt that now was the time to build places to hang out at after work. For pleasure and excitement, the idea of casinos began to bounce around the community.

After having a few talks with city officials, the potential owners discovered that it was going to be easy for them to get a liquor and gaming license. The interested residents quickly responded to this opportunity.

Aunt Mac said, "The gaming commission made it effortless because they knew that if the Westside had their own casinos, they would never have to worry about blacks visiting the casinos on Fremont Street or on the Strip."

New casinos opened, and the owners were black men. The casinos and owners were: the Cotton Club, James Calbert and Jodie Cannon; the El Morocco, Oscar Crozier; the Brown Derby, P.L. Jefferson; and the Elks Club, owned by the Elks' organization. The casinos were centrally located on Jackson Street, which placed them within walking distance of the majority of the homes. Jackson Street was to black folks what the strip was to whites.

Black people were starting to develop their own little Strip. They didn't agree with the segregated laws in Las Vegas. They simply felt that if you can't beat them, it might be easier to simply join them.

Now that the Westside was beginning to develop more businesses, there was a dire need for black workers such as dealers, waiters, waitresses, cooks and security guards.

Las Vegas is a twenty-four-hour city and practically every night was considered the weekend. On Wednesday nights, the Elks Club would have jam sessions and big-name entertainers like Pearl Bailey and Nat King Cole would stop by when they were in town to join in on the fun.

Regardless of how famous they were, the entertainers weren't allowed to stay or play at the Strip hotels they performed in. They also had to abide by the "no coloreds allowed" practice, which was in full force at all the business establishments on the Strip and downtown.

❧❧

While shopping in the community grocery store, a man accidentally bumped into Aunt Mac. He made a quick left turn that caused the carton of eggs she was carrying to fall on the floor. Constantly apologizing, the man knelt on the floor and began to wipe the front of her brand-new brown suede shoes. He knew they were ruined, so he offered to pay for the eggs and for the shoes.

Aunt Mac insisted he forget about the whole incident. As he continued to apologize, she took a closer look at him. All of a sudden, she noticed he was the boy she used to go with back home when she was fourteen years old. His name was Tom Tate.

Tom was a tall, dark and handsome black man with cute little dimples in the middle of his cheeks. He came to Las Vegas to work at the Basic Magnesium plant. He told her that when he left the sawmill in Mississippi, he promised he would never look back. Tom was a janitor at Hoover Dam.

Aunt Mac asked about the folks back home. She then looked down at his left hand to see if he had a wedding ring on, but the soiled handkerchief was in the way. She proceeded toward the cash register with a loaf of bread under her arm.

The curiosity of knowing whether he was married was starting to bother her. At the counter, she purposely pushed the bread so it would fall on the floor. Without hesitating, Tom picked up the loaf and carefully placed it on the counter. "You two finished?" the cashier said with sarcasm.

Aunt Mac ignored the comment and smiled as she looked at Tom's hand. No ring. As she opened her purse, Tom closed it and gave the cashier a crisp $20 bill. Little did Tom know, he had just passed two of Aunt Mac's most important tests: He wasn't married and he wasn't cheap.

Aunt Mac began dating Tom and he was the first man she became serious with after she arrived in Las Vegas. She said that because everyone knew each other, she had to be careful not to flirt with the wrong person.

Aunt Mac was very discreet and she simply did not want her business all over town. She said, "If I wanted anyone to know my doings, I would put it in the newspaper."

Aunt Mac and Tom's favorite hangout was the Cotton Club. The Cotton Club was named after the world-famous club in Harlem. But the Las Vegas version was not posh. It was merely an oversized room with a few craps tables, a bar, a jukebox in the corner, and a small stage for dancing or entertainment. A few large mirrors hung on the wall as well as autographed pictures of the owner with famous black and white entertainers.

The outside was just as dreary. The color of the building was off-white, and the club's name was neatly hand painted on the front. The only lights were located on the edges of the building. Aunt Mac said, "The only thing that made the Cotton Club posh was the people who frequented the place."

The Cotton Club attracted a more elite crowd. It was nothing to stop by and see entertainers hanging around, having a drink or performing a number on the small stage. The regulars were popular groups like the Ink Spots, the Treniers and the Mills Brothers.

One day she and Tom walked in and saw Cab Calloway, Billy Eckstine and Sammy Davis Jr. kissing and throwing dice at the craps table. They were talking loud, drinking and having a good time. They felt at home. From sunrise to sunset, the place was always crowded and jumping.

Aunt Mac could pretty much predict who would be in the club on a particular night. She would look in the paper and see who was headlining at the casinos and 90 percent of the time they would show up in the club after their last scheduled performance.

After six and a half months of dating, Aunt Mac decided to call it quits with Tom. She said she made it a rule to never date a man for more than six months without the intent of marriage. Tom told her that if she ever needed an escort to the clubs or church, to please do not hesitate to call.

Aunt Mac was the kind of woman who could walk into a place by herself and leave with three or four people. She felt that the only things anyone really needed in life were money and God.

She bought her first house and it was within walking distance of the clubs. She said that if by chance she had a drink too many, the only thing someone would have to do was to pick her up, walk a few feet and throw her on her doorstep.

Aunt Mac and Tom remained friends but she never had to call on him for his assistance.

In every town there are nosey people. When someone asked why she and Tom didn't get married, her response was always complete silence. Aunt Mac said, "Silence is golden and it always worked better than words."

1944, Magnolia and Tom Tate. Geran Family Collection

In 1947, Aunt Mac and the residents on the Westside were doing quite well. As planned, she was able to send her mama money every week, and because of her continuous generosity, her mama was able to save enough to buy a new car and a new winter coat.

After returning home from work, Aunt Mac opened a letter from her sister Rosa Lee stating that her mama was sick and that she should come home as soon as possible.

Dropping everything and notifying everyone who needed to know, Aunt Mac hopped in her new car and drove to Lexington.

With Aunt Mac's constant care, her mama began to feel better. She decided to head back home, but this time she wouldn't make the trip alone.

Her cousin, Lee Birda, not only wanted to help her drive her car, she wanted to get a taste of the city she had heard so much about. She said everyone who had left the South and moved to Las Vegas was sending a lot of money back to their folks and was supposedly living like kings and queens.

The minute they arrived in Las Vegas, Lee Birda discovered the rumors were true: Las Vegas did have a lot of potential. She decided to go back home, pack her few belongings and take the first bus for Las Vegas.

The day after she arrived, Lee Birda found a job. She was offered a position at the El Rancho Hotel in the laundry room earning $12 a day. Even though she knew there was segregation and unjust treatment of blacks in Las Vegas, it didn't bother her. It was practiced so much in Mississippi, she had grown accustomed to it.

෧৵৩

In 1935, the annual Helldorado Days were initiated and featured rodeos and mock gunfights. Because actors like Roy Rogers and others had made several cowboy movies about Nevada, Boulder City and Helldorado, the hotel-casino owners were convinced that the country and western flavor would best suit Las Vegas.

Lee Birda and her friend, Sue Brass, decided to attend the annual Helldorado Parade for the first time. When Lee Birda spotted a dark, husky man on a horse, she instantly became smitten. He was the only black cowboy participating in the event. He sat proudly on his big, black horse and was wearing the most beautiful boots she had ever seen.

Aunt Mac thought it was funny to hear about a black man riding a horse in the same parade the Klu Klux Klan once participated in. Although it had happened a few decades earlier, the terror of the event lingered in the minds of many of the black residents for quite some time.

An old-timer once told Aunt Mac that in 1924, a Klu Klux Klan parade was held on Fremont Street. After the parade, the fact that the white sheets were in town sent shock waves throughout the black community. They began to wonder, who among the town's whites could possibly be under those hoods?

It wasn't until one year later that the residents started to feel safe again, especially at night. The man responsible for this transition was the sixth mayor of Las Vegas, Fred Hesse. He vowed that such a parade would never take place again. But even with his promise, blacks realized the damage had been done.

Lee Birda nudged Sue in the side and asked if she knew who the handsome cowboy was. She said his name was Gold Dollar and that he was a close friend and bodyguard of a prominent Las Vegas casino owner, Benny Binion.

While Aunt Mac and Lee Birda were sitting in the keno lounge at the El Morocco Club, Gold Dollar walked in. Suddenly, Lee Birda became shy and refused to say anything to him. Aunt Mac thought she was silly. She walked over to Gold Dollar and grabbed him by the arm. She introduced herself and walked over to where Lee Birda was sitting and said, "This is Lee Birda." She then grabbed her drink and walked away.

After dating and messing around for six months, Lee and Dollar decided to marry.

Aunt Mac thought it was so cute how Gold Dollar proposed to Lee. He said, "Hey Birda, what you doing today?" She said, "Nothing. Why?" He smiled and while looking out the window he said, "'Cause us go get married." Lee Birda grabbed her purse and said, "Okay, let's go."

Gold Dollar with friend at the El Morroco Club. Rose Family Collection

Lee and Dollar went downtown to the courthouse to get their marriage certificate. Later that day, Lee called Mary Nettles and asked if they could get married in her house. She was honored. She immediately contacted all their friends and a beautiful ceremony took place.

Gold Dollar was known to kill "bad actors" for a fellow named Benny Binion. They were usually guys who tried to do harm to Binion or someone who didn't deserve it. In other words, when they disappeared, they weren't missed. Benny Binion and Gold Dollar used to hang out in the same neck of the woods back in Dallas, Texas. Dollar was from a nearby town called Victoria, and Binion was from Dallas.

Aunt Mac said Binion brought Gold Dollar with him to Las Vegas. It was said that Dollar saved Binion's life once, a topic he never discussed with anybody. Since then, they had been inseparable.

When Lee Birda and Gold Dollar had their first and only child, they named him after Binion, Leslie Benny Rose. While waiting for their home on the Westside to go through escrow (a gift from Benny), Binion allowed them to stay in the servant quarters of his mansion. Lee Birda loved it because all she had to do was take care of her baby. For the first time she had a maid to do all her work.

There was one incident, however, at the mansion that caused a little fright in Lee. Early one morning, while walking out the front door, she heard a ripple of gunshots nearby. It turned out to be two men in a speeding car shooting at Binion as he was getting out of his car. They missed but not by much. Binion waited until he couldn't see the car anymore, walked inside, ate his breakfast and came back out to ride his horse that Gold Dollar had named Nigger.

Binion made his millions from running illegal gambling houses and bootlegging liquor in Dallas. Dollar said Binion never worried about going broke. When he needed money, he would go out and rob the other bootleggers in town. He knew they wouldn't go to the cops because their operations were illegitimate.

The rumor around town was that Binion killed three people, two in Dallas and one in Las Vegas. He only admitted to one. Binion was called the "Kingpin" of crime in Dallas. His FBI record went back as far as 1924 and the crimes were said to have been unimaginable. Binion's motto was "kill 'em dead and they won't give you no more trouble."

The people of Las Vegas were a little shocked when the Nevada Tax Commission issued him a gaming license to operate a casino. The Tax Commission said Binion promised that he would not run a gaming house in another state. The board trusted "his word" and therefore a license was granted.

When Binion started the Horseshoe, he never forgot his friends, especially the ones who spent time behind bars on his behalf. No matter how long they were away, he still remembered. Binion was never convicted of any of the murders he was said to have committed. And Gold Dollar was never a suspect.

Benny Binion knew he had a bad reputation in town and he wanted to make sure his enemies wouldn't try to rob him. His solution was to hire them.

Benny Binion and Gold Dollar. Rose Family Collection

It was said that Binion had employed in his casino all the thieves in Las Vegas. He taught them the business, "do this and don't do that," and not to his surprise, they became his best workers.

Aunt Mac said Binion was also the kind of man who would loan a mere acquaintance a thousand dollars without making him put up any type of security. He had been known to hand you the money and say something as sincere as "just pay it when you can, son."

Aunt Mac believed that Binion's down-to-earth personality was the reason his casino was so successful.

Gold Dollar was known as being one of the few black cowboys in Las Vegas and in the state of Nevada. He produced the All Colored Rodeo, which toured the continent. The poster that advertised the event read:

World Championship
All Colored Rodeo
White and Colored Welcome
Gold Dollar Rose
Producer

$700 Prize Money

Saddle Bronco, Bareback Riding, Calf Roping
Steer Wrestling, Bull Riding
Night Show Only - 8 p.m.
Children 75¢ Adults $1.25

Gold Dollar, whose birth name was Perry Rose, got his name after winning a rodeo contest in Europe. The prize "purse" contained hundreds of solid gold, one-dollar coins.

When he and the guys came back to the States, they went on tour in New York. On their last night at the rodeo, he purchased ten cases of liquor and poured every drop into a big wooden barrel. He then threw in a handful of gold coins. The guys grabbed the nearest cups and began dipping for the coins and liquor and started shouting, "Gold dollar, gold dollar." Since then his family and the people in the community started calling him by his well deserved name.

Feeling obligated to live up to his name, Gold Dollar decided to create a trademark for himself. He had all of his teeth, the top and bottom, capped in gold.

When Aunt Mac notified her cousins, Erwin and Hazel, in Chicago that cousin Lee Birda had married a cowboy with gold teeth, their curiosity about Las Vegas was piqued. They couldn't wait to give this much-talked-about city a try. Aunt Mac sent Lee Birda on the train to Chicago to make sure Hazel and Erwin arrived safely.

Hazel and Erwin lately had been seriously thinking about leaving the "Windy City." They were born in Lexington, Mississippi, but decided to move with their mama's sister in Chicago.

When Hazel was thirteen and Erwin was fifteen, their mama died. While growing up, they lived with several relatives, but their favorite was Aunt Mac.

Aunt Mac spent a great deal of time with them. She would take time to explain things and show them how to do the chores around the house, mainly because she didn't want to do them herself.

They began to look at her as a mother figure rather than an older cousin. Her comforting words of advice made it possible for them to get through a lot of emotional and frustrating days.

When Lee Birda arrived in Chicago, she stayed up all night bragging about how great things were in Las Vegas. Erwin had already heard a few tales of the Westside prior to Lee's renditions and was already sold that it was the place for him.

Hazel had just lost her job. The company she worked for was forced to close its doors due to a lack of funds, so the move would be very beneficial.

The next day, Erwin drove his car to Las Vegas and was transporting Aunt Mac's most prized jewels, her family.

Erwin's nickname was Brother. He was a fair-skinned black man with straight black hair. The folks back home thought he favored Babe Ruth, but he thought he looked more like Elvis Presley. Aunt Mac couldn't understand why he chose Elvis as his idol, because he couldn't dance a lick.

Ever since Erwin was a teenager, one of his major goals in life was to never get married. He felt it was too confining.

The day Erwin arrived in Las Vegas he immediately went to the Horseshoe to meet this man named Gold Dollar. All the way from Chicago, Lee Birda talked so much about him that Erwin couldn't wait to meet him.

Gold Dollar introduced him to Benny Binion. Binion said that he noticed him looking around at the slot machines and asked if he knew how to repair them. Erwin said he didn't have any idea. Binion said, "Good, now go to the office and tell them I said to put you to work."

Erwin Wilburn, Lee Birda Rose, L.B. Gibbs and Hazel Geran at the Cotton Club. Geran Family Collection

After being in Las Vegas for two days, Erwin was hired as a slot machine mechanic at the Horseshoe.

Even though he didn't have a clue about how to repair the "one-armed bandits," he reported to work the next day. The mechanics at the hotel were all white and although Erwin was a fair-complexioned black man with straight black hair, he was still considered a "darky."

Erwin said at first none of the guys would show him what to do. So he began to open up the machines and teach himself how to repair them. He believed that if you set your mind to something, you could do it. He really needed the job and he was willing to make whatever sacrifices were necessary to keep it. He liked Binion but he loved working around all that money.

Hazel thought the people on the Westside were friendly and the men were plentiful, which was one of the reasons Aunt Mac did not stay with one man for a long period of time. She said, "There were too many options in the sea."

Hazel's first job was domestic work. A year later, in 1949, she applied as a keno writer at the Cotton Club. Because the require-

Keno writers at the Cotton Club, Hazel Geran and Bessie Colbert. Geran Family Collection

ments a girl had to have included being pretty and young, Hazel had the job the moment she walked in the door. The pay was $3.75 an hour.

A nice-looking gentleman began to drop by the Cotton Club for a drink and to play a little keno. A few weeks later, Hazel noticed that his visits became every day. He began flirting with her from a distance.

Finally, he walked over to her station and introduced himself. His name was Johnus and he was new in town. He was born in Baton Rouge, Louisiana, but had been living in San Francisco, California, for the past nine years.

Johnus had just completed barber school and received his license from the state of Nevada. He was having the vacant office space across the street transformed into a barbershop.

Aunt Mac said Hazel liked men who wanted their own businesses. It made her feel safe and secure.

Johnus's observation of Hazel as she mixed and mingled with her customers began to be a ritual. What was odd about him was when it was time for her shift to end he made sure he was nowhere to be seen. Aunt Mac told Hazel that although he seemed aggressive, he really was shy so she might have to make a move.

When Hazel discovered the Cotton Club was about to change management, she knew a layoff was around the corner. She decided that instead of looking for another job, she would look for Johnus. Hazel wasn't shy when it came to getting what she wanted.

After four weeks of dating and being seen around town as a couple, Hazel and Johnus were married. After getting their marriage license downtown, later that evening they invited a few close friends over for a sit-down dinner at Aunt Mac's little house.

Johnus had heard about Las Vegas from his friend Jim Roberts. Jim earned the nickname Gentleman Jim by never getting angry even when it was appropriate. When he got mad he was still nice, and he exerted his anger in the most subtle ways. People

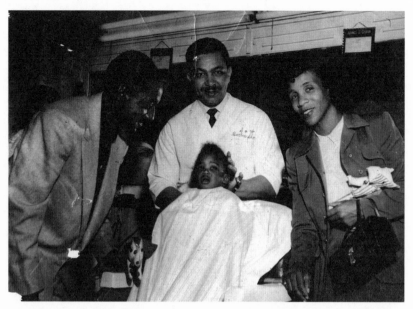

Sportsman Barber shop, owner/barber Johnus Geran gives a little boy his first haircut. Geran Family Collection

were amazed at how cool he remained even when matters unraveled for the worse right before his eyes.

Jim had owned a bar in San Francisco's Filmore District and Johnus was a barber in the shop next door. When Jim left the Bay Area to find work in Las Vegas, Johnus began to think about a change of scenery as well.

Johnus opened one of the few barbershops on Jackson Street. It was called Sportsman Barber Shop and the name was derived from one of his passions, hunting.

Most of the black residents in Las Vegas loved hunting. Quail, geese, deer, pheasant and rabbits were the most sought-after animals. After trying a few places on the outskirts of town, they finally found the perfect grounds to hunt in Elko, Nevada, a small town more than 400 miles north of Las Vegas.

Upon their return, they would go to one of the hunter's back yards and clean the animals. A clothesline was used to hang the furs or skins that were removed. They would have their wives marinate the meat for a few hours, then have it baked or fried.

Fishing was also popular and the area the residents used the most was around Hoover Dam.

Golfing was another favorite sport, but only a few black residents knew how to play. The first black golf club was Valley View Golf Club. It was organized and co-founded by Jim Roberts and Filbert Cobbs. The only golf course they were allowed to play was Las Vegas Municipal, which was near the Westside.

Most of the Valley View members migrated to Las Vegas from the West Coast, and they were already established golfers. Aunt Mac said, "You can best believe that they were some white man's caddy before they became a golfer. The only way they could learn how to swing was to sneak on the course when no one was around, and they learned how to keep score by simply watching and listening."

Aunt Mac dated one of the members. His name was George Moore. Every once in a while she would join him on the course and play a nine-hole game. After a few weeks of courting, she got tired of golfing and George and decided to swing him out of her life.

Valley View Golf Club members. Geran Family Collection

Valley View Golf Club dinner celebration. Geran Family Collection

She said, "At that time, there were so many available black men in Las Vegas a woman could date several at one time without causing any kind of ruckus."

Aunt Mac once successfully dated seven men at the same time. She sat each one of them down and explained that she was only a friend to all of the men in her life. They understood and they knew she was sincere and honest about it.

Her house was not very spacious and it truly was a miracle how she managed to keep a fair amount of distance between the men's visits. It was said to be so small that when she stepped in the front door she was almost out the back. But regardless of the size of her house, one can't help but notice that Aunt Mac was simply a "natural" when it came to handling men.

While dating these guys, Aunt Mac told each of them that she wanted to surprise her childhood friend Ella for her birthday. Ella lived in Harlem, in New York, and Aunt Mac wanted so much

Magnolia and Pete McCoy, her fifth husband. Geran Family Collection

to see her. After a few days of casually mentioning the trip, two of the guys out of the seven offered to accompany her. The day before Ella's birthday, Aunt Mac was on a plane to New York with two of her gentlemen friends.

After the trip, Aunt Mac considered the two men as finalists. After a few months of dating, the one she decided to marry was the one who waited the longest for her. His name was Pete McCoy.

Pete was her fifth husband and she wanted him to be the last, but in less than a month things got rocky and the marriage lasted only a year. Aunt Mac said, "He had the nerve to become jealous of my other men friends. And they say women change after they marry. I think men are just as bad."

Chapter

The Color of Money
"When the white man does something to one of us, he has done it to us all."

The first time Aunt Mac drove down the Strip, in 1943, not only did she notice there wasn't a black person in sight, she noticed that the names on the hotel marquees were those of white entertainers.

In 1941, the El Rancho Vegas opened. It was the first hotel-casino-showroom combination with 110 rooms, an it was the most modern hotel built with a ranch style and western décor. During its first year, the entertainment in the showroom was strictly country and western. They were called cowboy casinos. Aunt Mac said the floors were sprinkled with sawdust and donkeys were sometimes used as part of the act.

The popular western entertainers appeared not only at the El Rancho but at the downtown hotels as well. Fremont Street had its own hotel industry. It had the Apache Hotel and the Arizona Club and a few others. Altogether there were 200 rooms.

Soon after, the casinos began to discover that not everyone who came to Las Vegas was interested in gambling and drinking. When couples arrived in town, the men gambled while their wives attended the shows.

There was a short period when black people were able to frequent the casinos downtown and on the Strip. The reason they rarely visited the El Rancho was because the prices were so high.

The hotel appealed to people who had the luxury of spending without worrying about the amount.

Las Vegas gradually was replacing San Francisco as the place where the Hollywood types could come to escape from the rat race in Los Angeles.

Occasionally, there were acts that featured movie stars. Hollywood, during those years, had contract players who were expected to act as well as sing and dance. But Las Vegas was already overloaded with acts like the Sons of the Lone Frontier, Jimmy Wakeley and other cowboys.

One year after the El Rancho's debut, the Last Frontier opened in 1942. It was located farther to the south, a mile from the El Rancho. The Last Frontier had 107 rooms and was the first place visitors from Southern California would see when they hit town and the last when they departed.

During the first two years, the Last Frontier had country and western entertainment and its decor was Southwestern. The other hotels decided to follow the same format in order to keep up.

The day finally came when the Strip and downtown hotels had to take a closer look at the black entertainers. They began to realize they would have to offer something different if they wanted to beat their out-of-state competitors. Because gaming was pretty much the same in all of the casinos, they predicted that entertainment would become the drawing card.

In 1944, the El Cortez on Fremont Street presented the Deep River Boys. It was the first large hotel with colored entertainment. A year later, the Last Frontier introduced Tip Tap Toe, a trio of colored tap-dancers. For several months these groups performed to full houses and that's when the hotel owners realized that black entertainment could generate the level of interest and cash flow they were looking for.

It was said that Benjamin "Bugsy" Siegel was the master-mind behind the Flamingo Hotel but this is not true. During the early 1940s, the publisher of the *Hollywood Reporter*, W. R. "Billy" Wilkerson, frequented Las Vegas to feed his compulsion and fulfill his number one passion — gambling.

While riding to the airport he spotted a "For Sale" sign on a 33-acre lot. He took the number and immediately called his lawyer, Greg Bautzer, to negotiate a deal for him. Billy was aware that practically everyone in town knew he was a high-roller and if word got out that he was the one inquiring about the land, the price might double or maybe even triple.

The owner was Margaret Folsom, a bordello owner in Hawaii, who was down on her luck. Greg Bautzer, a handsome playboy law-yer, was able to talk Margaret into selling the land for $84,000.

The location was perfect. It was at the south end of the Strip; it was on the main highway into town but it wasn't close enough to the other casinos to be considered competition, a situation Wilkerson definitely wanted to avoid.

Wilkerson was known to gamble at least $150,000 a year. He loved craps, poker and the track. On numerous occasions he gambled the *Hollywood Reporter's* payroll. He began to grow tired of losing and he loathed borrowing from banks. As a solution to his problems, Billy Wilkerson decided to build his own casino in Las Vegas.

Billy was a lover of exotic birds, so much so that he named his hotel the Flamingo. He wanted to bring Paris to Las Vegas and he envisioned pink flamingos walking around the premises. He insisted there be no windows or clocks because he wanted his guest to "lose themselves" while gambling. The employees were to wear evening attire, tuxes and tails, and the rooms were to have central air conditioning. Billy envisioned Sunset Strip in the desert. He was a very organized and professional, savvy business-man who only hired the best in their fields to be on his staff. His biggest flaw, however, was gambling. The more money he raised for his project, the more he gambled. After many ups and downs and even more failed attempts, Billy gave up and realized that Las Vegas was not the place for him. For some reason, he thought the obligations of the hotel-casino would ease a little if he could just double the money at the craps table. His winnings versus his losses were devastating.

Billy decided to call "the Boys," Moe Sedway and Gus Greenbaum, the owners of the El Cortez Hotel. He told them Las Vegas was not good for him and he would like them to complete his hotel. For close to a year, the Flamingo sat unfinished. "The Boys" decided to call Meyer Lansky and he in turn assigned a man he knew thought of Las Vegas as a place with great potential. His name was Benjamin "Bugsy" Siegel. He was Wilkerson's new partner and the financial backers for the project would be the Nevada Project Corporation, also known as Murder, Inc.

Murder, Inc. used the Nevada Project Corporation to pour mob money into the accounts. Siegel was then able to retrieve the funds legally without raising the eyebrows of various police officials.

Like Wilkerson, in the early '40s Ben Siegel was often seen at the El Rancho and Last Frontier making enormous bets on the crap tables. Most of the gossip about Ben Siegel was either in the newspaper or just common talk around town. When he tried to purchase the El Cortez Hotel, everyone in town knew that because of his criminal background, city officials made it clear they would see to it that he would never become an owner of a casino in their town.

Wilkerson informed Siegel that because the location was outside the city limits, they could retrieve water from a well, generate their own power and would not need the city's assistance. Ben loved this news. Now he could finally tell the city guys to kiss off.

Meyer Lansky knew that Ben Siegel had recognized the possibilities for making big money in Las Vegas for many years. When

Ben first told his partners in crime that he saw gold in the middle of the desert, they thought he was crazy. But this time, Meyer Lansky needed Ben to follow through with Wilkerson's vision.

At first Ben enjoyed being around such an elegant guy as Billy but in a short time he became resentful, which eventually turned into a jealous rage. Ben hated the fact that the Flamingo was Billy's baby and not his. He wanted all the credit.

Ben Siegel began to make numerous business dealings without Billy's knowledge. The budget was out of control. He had overspent by 400 percent. What was once a project budgeted by Billy at a little under $1,200,000 was now a nightmare. These "stories" got back to "the Boys" at the Nevada Project Corporation and they immediately demanded that Siegel show them a financial statement.

Ben turned to Billy for help by asking him to give up his shares in the project. When Billy refused, Ben threatened to kill him. At the advice of his lawyer, Greg Bautzer, Billy fled for his life to Paris.

Operating under extreme pressure from "the Boys," Ben Siegel decided to open the Flamingo even though the hotel rooms were not ready. On December 26, 1946, the casino opened and became the third major establishment on the Strip, joining the El Rancho and Last Frontier.

"Bugsy" Siegel of Murder, Inc. Special Collections, UNLV Library

Front portico of Flamingo Hotel. Special Collections, UNLV Library

Flamingo Hotel's swimming pool in 1946. Special Collections, UNLV Library

The grand opening was a glittering premiere in true Hollywood style. Ben Siegel intended it to be comparable to Monte Carlo and as lavish as the resorts in Miami.

On the night of the opening, Aunt Mac's neighbor, Peve, an 18-year-old, asked his friend Moe Sedway, the nephew of Moe Greene, a prominent casino businessman and a well-known mob figure, if he could valet cars for the Flamingo. Sedway received the okay from one of the hotel's top brass and he agreed that they could use the extra help.

Peve wasn't asked to fill out an application. He was given a uniform to wear and was told to report for work at 7 p.m. and whatever tips he made that night were his pay.

The residents on the Westside thought Peve was brave to have a friend ask a gangster for a job, but crazy when he asked his friend Harry to assist him at the event. Everybody knew Harry couldn't drive.

Peve said he would stop by the club after work to let them know how the night went. What everybody really wanted to know was how many cars did Harry crash? It was forecast to rain all night and it didn't look like Peve's decision to ask for Harry's help was a good one.

When Peve walked through the club's door there was a great sense of relief. He was so proud he had earned $75 in such a short period of time. Never in his life had he earned that much money in one day. The roll was so big it was bulging out of his pocket. When he went home to change, his father saw the wad of money on top of his dresser drawer, and immediately asked, "Who have you done robbed?"

Peve said there were so many movie stars at the event he thought he was on a studio lot in Hollywood. On one hand it seemed unreal but on the other it was so perfectly orchestrated.

Although many of the invited guests did not show up because of the cancellation of flights due to wet weather, it was a night Peve would remember for the rest of his life.

For a whole month, Peve bragged about how much money he was getting parking cars at the Flamingo. One day he went to work and discovered that another black man was in his position.

Apparently the man knew someone connected with the hotel and a phone call was made on his behalf. Later that day he was the new valet parking attendant. Peve was devastated.

Peve told Aunt Mac that he learned a valuable lesson and now he knows when to keep his mouth shut. Her response to him was, "Never tell people how much you make, especially when it involves tips. Those one-dollar bills can add up to an unbelievable amount."

Peve's next job was at the Last Frontier. He was hired as a bar boy. After being on the job for forty-five days, he was fired for showing up late.

The next day, Peve went to work and acted like nothing ever happened. The shift supervisor said, "I thought I got rid of you?" Peve answered, "Yes, you did, but that was yesterday. Today is another day." The man shook his head and walked away and Peve continued to stack the bar with clean glasses.

Jimmy Durante and Xavier Cugat headlined and played on the same bill at the Flamingo for the first two weeks. But even with top acts like these, the hotel experienced a tremendous loss.

At times there were only around nine or ten guests in the showrooms. The initial amount Murder, Inc. agreed to loan Bugsy was $1 million. After the opening, he was given a specified number of days to pay the difference of the $5.6 million.

In early January of 1947, Lena Horne replaced Jimmy Durante, and Xavier Cugat and his orchestra was the band she was to perform with. She was the first black entertainer to perform at the Flamingo and miraculously was the first to stay there as well. Her show ran for two weeks.

Aunt Mac had a friend who was a maid at the hotel. Everyone knew that Lena Horne didn't care much for Xavier Cugat. She thought he was a real jerk. He was snide and rude when he introduced her and he didn't rehearse or discipline his band. Finally Lena was fed up and was ready to walk out the door.

She called her husband, Lennie, in Southern California and said she was ready to quit. Lennie called the manager but he didn't want to hear any complaints. He then reminded them that they were under contract and it was not meant to be broken.

Lennie decided to go over the manager's head and contact the real man in charge. After numerous unsuccessful attempts, he finally got in touch with Bugsy Siegel. When

Lena Horne and husband, Lennie Hayton, at the Flamingo in 1947. Las Vegas News Bureau

Siegel heard how Lena was being treated, he sent a couple of his boys to have a talk with Xavier. At the next show, Lena was introduced like a queen.

The black residents of Las Vegas knew Lena didn't care much for the city. She experienced a number of discomforting incidents that mostly involved acts of racism or unjust treatment by white residents and hotel executives. Although Lena was privileged to stay at the hotel, she was not allowed to enter the casino or use any other areas in the hotel.

Places on the Westside were not inviting and she wouldn't dare lower herself by going to the theaters or other public places that were segregated. She was in fact confined to her bungalow.

Whenever she came to the Westside to one of the clubs, some-one was bound to piss her off. Lena was known to tell somebody a thing or two. She could curse like a sailor.

Nevertheless, Lena continued to come back to Las Vegas for the next decade or so. Las Vegas paid better than any of the other clubs and it was probably the reason she tolerated the unjust and unpleasant atmosphere. Her visits to Las Vegas eventually stopped.

Pearl Bailey was treated just the opposite of Lena. During her performances at the Flamingo in 1947, she was told she had to find a place to stay on the Westside. She could perform at the Flamingo, but she couldn't sleep there.

The residents often wondered why Lena was able to stay and Pearl was not. They were both superstars. Blacks in Las Vegas concluded that it must have been because of the color of her skin. A former maid at the Flamingo named Ina Mae Cooks believed that because Pearl was much darker than Lena, the Southern white guests accepted Lena as an "almost white" person and Pearl as be-ing just another black.

Pearl Bailey on stage at Flamingo in 1947.
Special Collections, UNLV Library

Ben Siegel's clien-tele included many of the Hollywood types and Lena was looked upon as a star rather than just a black female performer. These are the only excuses the residents could justify why there was different treatment between the two performers.

Pearl was ob-sessed with having

her dressing table set the night before and after her performance and the maids were well aware of that.

One night, Pearl came into her dressing room to get ready for her first show and discovered her vanity table had been turned upside down. Her make-up was scattered all over the floor and her tablecloth was missing. She told the maid to go and get the manager.

Pearl Bailey on stage at the El Rancho in 1948. Las Vegas News Bureau

The manager walked in and told Pearl that he was sorry for the mess but the reason for it was because they needed to take the tablecloth. Mr. Siegel wanted everything accounted for. The manager then promised he would send another one right over.

The next night it happened again. Pearl demanded to see Mr. Siegel after the show. To everyone's surprise, especially the hotel's management, Bugsy came backstage and waited until Pearl's show was over.

When Pearl passed by him, she nodded and continued walking. He then grabbed her arm and said, "Did you ask to see me?" But Pearl continued walking to her dressing room and Mr. Siegel followed like she was the boss.

Pearl entered her dressing room and her maid immediately began mixing a tall martini. With her knees knocking and her hands trembling, the maid poured the contents into a chilled glass and handed it to Pearl.

Pearl took a sip and said, "Are you Bugsy Siegel?" He responded, "My friends call me Benjamin, my enemies call me Bugsy." She proceeded to tell him that all she wanted was one measly fresh tablecloth to be on her table the night before each performance. Siegel, calm and cool, said, "Is that all? Anything else?" Pearl, now on her second drink, said, "Well, since you asked. I would like a fire engine red Road Master Buick. I'm tired of bumming a ride to the show every night. My car is in L.A. and cabs don't run on the Westside. So how about it? My mama always told me that a closed mouth can't get fed."

The next day, when Pearl walked into her dressing room, the tablecloths were piled high on top of the table and after the show when she arrived at Mrs. Harrison's house, the place where she rented a room, the red Buick she asked for was sitting in the front with the keys in the ignition.

For months, the whole town talked about Pearl and Siegel. It was said to have been her best performance.

Pearl Bailey's reaction to Benjamin Siegel said quite a bit about the relationship between black entertainers and the newly developing hotel industry in Las Vegas. Even though Pearl's wishes were granted, she feared Siegel and she wouldn't do anything that would have angered him. She knew he decided which black entertainer he wanted to play and stay in his hotel and she knew not to question him.

The Flamingo attracted a different clientele than the other hotels. While it was true Siegel was personally associated with the acting colony of Hollywood and even some of Europe's royalty, a large portion of his clientele were from back East or were the new rich oil tycoons from Texas and Louisiana. The oil tycoons had serious reservations regarding blacks. They believed separate was equal, whereas the visitors from the East Coast were biased toward racism.

The Flamingo also brought a new kind of entertainment to Las Vegas. The New York bunch wanted the sort of entertainment that was popular in New York's cafe society. Their favorite pastime was to go slumming to the Cotton Club of Harlem to catch some of the best black entertainment.

It was said that Virginia Hill, Siegel's girlfriend, once owned an interest in the Cotton Club and had some input in what acts should perform there. At the Flamingo, she was able to call those same shots. She definitely had a say in who performed behind the satin curtains in the showroom.

Between January and October, the Flamingo Hotel's policy began to change. When Pearl Bailey returned, she was now able to stay and play and join the list of other performers of the brown race, Lena Horne and Arthur Lee Simpkins. Regardless of her mistreatment in the beginning, she still thought Las Vegas was an elegant place and she was happy for the change.

Aunt Mac thought Ben Siegel was a funny yet serious character. One day, she had the pleasure of running into him in the Flamingo's kitchen. She was waiting for her boyfriend, John, a cook at the time, to finish his shift. He was a very fair-skinned man with straight hair and she didn't think management knew he was black.

John said that his white co-workers would talk and laugh about black folks while he was in the room. He said every day there was a darky joke or racist comment made. Sometimes they would laugh so hard, their faces would turn red as a tomato. John explained to Aunt Mac that was why the workers suddenly became quiet every time she walked in.

Bugsy Siegel walked up to Aunt Mac and introduced himself. He then asked her what color was her pretty sweater. She took a guess and said, "I think it's blue gray." He laughed and walked away with four of the biggest bodyguards she had ever seen.

Aunt Mac had several close encounters with Siegel but that was the first time they had exchanged words. She said, "He was kind, with a cute baby face. He sure didn't look like a murderer, but then again, what does a murderer look like?"

Aunt Mac wanted so much to tell Siegel they had a common interest, that their lawyer was Louis Wiener, but she never had the courage. He always appeared to be busy and she didn't want to intrude on his valuable time.

Louis "Louie" Wiener Jr. had an all-star list of clients. Frank Sinatra and Bugsy Siegel, as well as other prominent mob figures, were among those he represented. At that time, there were only a few lawyers in town. Because of his sincere character, the blacks in Las Vegas chose Louie Wiener to represent them.

Louie was Jewish. Aunt Mac loved him and he was crazy about her. When she called Louie it was always for the same reason: for him to arrange a quickie divorce from her husband "of the month." When Aunt Mac called Louie to tell him that she no longer wanted to be married to Pete McCoy, her fifth husband, Louie replied, "My goodness, Magnolia, what are you trying to do, catch up with the movie stars?" Six months later she married Jimmy Neal, her sixth husband. He waited two years for her.

All she had to do was call Louie at his office and he would reassure her that everything was handled. Louie made law deals and did business with a handshake and everyone knew that his word was good.

Benjamin Siegel, like Wilkerson, not only wanted his place to be the best-looking hotel and casino, he expected his employees to follow the same policy. He was so particular about the workers' appearance that he developed a dress code. The new uniform for the employees, and that included the janitors, was a formal tuxedo. He wanted the place to be classy in every way.

John said one morning, while walking across the patio, Siegel spotted a man wearing a tuxedo, stretched out on a chaise lounge chair. Bugsy ran over and kicked viciously at the chair, yelling, "What the hell are you doing? Get back to work, you bum, before I boot your ass." The man sat up in the chair, with his eyes popping out of his head and said, "But-but," he stammered, "I'm a g-g-guest."

Magnolia and Jimmy Neal, her sixth husband. Geran Family Collection

Siegel was noted for that kind of behavior and he was also known to carry a gun at all times just in case he had to act on his threats. He knew that most of the other hotel owners cared nothing for him. They felt that because he was a gangster, he gave Las Vegas a bad reputation, the kind that would be hard for a new city to overcome. On the contrary, the blacks in Las Vegas thought his gangster image and style brought more notoriety and excitement to the city.

Siegel went out of his way to create the illusion that the Flamingo was a respectable place. He was concerned about who entered "his" hotel and how comfortable they were. He wasn't about to allow anyone to make his place look like a dive and he took all the necessary precautions to guard against this ever happening.

The single-minded Siegel was also determined to run his undertaking with proper decorum. To ensure that his property was maintained, Bugsy hired some of the beefiest musclemen the mob could provide. He wanted law and order and the ability to throw out anybody who was drunk or who was known to be a troublemaker.

But Ben Siegel was not able to regain his losses and this infuriated Murder, Inc. On March 19, 1947, Billy Wilkerson sold his shares in the Flamingo Hotel for $600,000. He initially asked for $2 million but he received the "take what you get" offer. On June 20, 1947, Benjamin "Bugsy" Siegel was shot repeatedly while sitting in the living room of Virginia Hill's mansion in Beverly Hills, California.

Blacks in Las Vegas mourned Siegel's death. They liked his style and felt he was good for Las Vegas' image. Aunt Mac said, "He was our golden boy."

↾↽

From the plushest Strip casino to the tiniest downtown dive, the blacks in Las Vegas knew there were imaginary "no colored allowed" signs hanging on every corner. Although entertainers and workers were allowed in the hotels and casinos and in some of the business establishments, they were told to don't even think about dropping a nickel in a slot machine.

When the gangsters from the north and back East began working in the hotels, they didn't want any "Nigrahs" upsetting their high-rolling, Southern gentlemen clients who had more oil wells than they had slot machines. Many of the mobsters had been brought up in slums and they had frequent fights with colored gangs. When they arrived, they were already filled with prejudice and hatred.

Black entertainers weren't publicly vocal about the discrimination they encountered, mainly because they knew it was happening all around the United States.

When Louis Armstrong traveled through the South, he said the food was awful and on many nights, they would stay up looking for a place where they could cook. They carried a bunch of pots and pans around with them and if they had a colored bus driver, it was common for the police to arrest him for speeding, even though he was traveling at the proper limit.

The northwest was no different. Every town had its own form of segregation. When Aunt Mac and her girlfriend June were sitting at the bar in the Cotton Club, Will, from the Will Mastin Trio, said they found Spokane, Washington, the same as Cab Calloway found New Orleans, a racist place.

On one particular stay in Spokane, Will came into the dressing room, flopped into the chair, and said, "Well, I've covered every street downtown. Nothing." He started taking off his shoes, rubbing his feet. "Tomorrow I'll go back over to Mrs. Clark's and see if she's expecting anything to open up. Meantime, guess we'll have to sleep in here."

"You mean there is nothing in the whole city of Spokane?" his son, Sammy Davis Jr., asked. "There ain't that many colored rooming houses to start with," responded Will. Growing more and more impatient, Sammy said, "What about a hotel? Ain't a single colored hotel around? A colored side of town? Colored rooming house? Colored hotels? Colored, colored, colored."

Aunt Mac and June laughed at how funny Will sounded. It was obvious Jim Crow laws existed everywhere black folks went, and Las Vegas was no exception.

When Sammy Davis Jr. and the Will Mastin Trio arrived in Las Vegas, little did they know a similar experience that they had in Spokane was waiting for them.

The Trio received the news that they were booked as the opening act at the El Rancho for $500 a week. For the first time, they felt like they had hit the big time.

When the Trio arrived backstage at the El Rancho, the band was the biggest they had ever seen. The floor was springy and slick and the lighting was modern. Then the question about their room was asked. The manager informed them they couldn't stay in the hotel. Sammy immediately picked up his suitcase and told his dad that he was ready to go.

Sammy and the Trio decided to catch a cab and drive around until they could locate a place to stay. The cab driver, a white man, informed them that a woman named Mrs. Cartwright had rooms for rent on the Westside. The cab stopped in front of a decent-looking house and they were so relieved.

Sammy thought the Westside looked like "Tobacco Road." They had just passed by a three-year-old girl standing naked in front of a shack made of wooden crates. It was unfit for human life. He prayed that this was not where they had to stay.

When the cab driver began pulling out their luggage, Mrs. Cartwright stood in the doorway waving. She then walked up to the driver and handed him a rolled up twenty-dollar bill.

Mrs. Cartwright politely said, "You boys with one of the shows? Well, I got three nice rooms for you." She then told them the price per night. Will was shocked. He said, "But that's probably twice what it would cost at the El Rancho Vegas." Mrs. Cartwright responded, "Then why don't you go live at the El Rancho?"

Tired, beat down and anxious to perform, Sammy said to just pay her the money. Will started counting out loud what the first week's rent would be. He smiled at Mrs. Cartwright and sarcastically said, "Looks like if the ofays don't get us, then our own will." "Business is business, I've got my own troubles." she said.

The law of supply and demand was in effect and Mrs. Cartwright knew she had the Will Mastin Trio in the palm of her hands. When other black entertainers, big names or not, stopped by to ask about the price to rent a room, they received the same treatment.

Mrs. Cartwright charged Sammy and the Will Mastin Trio $15 per room a night. The El Rancho charged only $4.

On the Trio's first night at the El Rancho, while waiting for the second show, Sammy thought it would be fun to take a look around the casino. He had $50 he wanted to make into $100. Will decided to join him.

When Sammy opened the casino's door, he and Will could hardly believe their eyes. There was so much excitement and noise from the clanging of slot machines, the piercing screams of people, and the uttering of dealers, to the liveliest music playing in the background, they thought they were in another world.

Sammy smiled like a kid in a candy store and turned to his father. Suddenly a hand appeared on his shoulder. It was a security guard. He shook his head and they knew what that meant. Sammy was so disappointed. He thought that since they were performing at the hotel, they could receive differential treatment, at least until their contract was up.

The most humiliating story Aunt Mac had ever heard about a big-name star in Las Vegas involved Sammy Davis Jr. After their first night at the El Rancho, Sammy decided to head home to Mrs. Cartwright's. He was trying to stay out of trouble. He thought a good movie would ease his mind, so he headed out the door and walked downtown to the theater.

After buying a bag of popcorn, he walked down the aisle and sat in the front row. Suddenly, a hand grabbed his arm and yanked him out of his seat, dragging him halfway down the aisle and out to the lobby. He looked up and saw that it was a sheriff's deputy with a big western hat on.

He asked Sammy, "What are you, boy, a wise guy?" Then he slapped Sammy across the face and said, "Speak up when I talk to you." Slowly, Sammy responded, "What'd I do?" Looking him straight in the eyes, the sheriff said, "Coloreds sit in the last three rows. You're in Nevada now, not New York. Mind our rules and you'll be treated square. Now go on back and enjoy the movie, boy."

When the blacks on the Westside heard about the incident, they felt bad. Aunt Mac said, "It was a shame that a star was treated just like another nigger."

The black residents believed in the old Southern saying, "When the white man does something to one of us, he has done it to us all." Sammy's incident created a great deal of discomfort and pain in the community.

ക്ക

Toward the end of the '40s, things began to change, but only by a fraction. Most of the black entertainers who were privileged to stay in the hotel rooms and eat in the restaurants discovered they were no longer welcomed after their contracts were completed. On rare occasions, if they wanted to continue staying at the hotels where they performed, sep-arate quarters were provided.

The El Rancho offered individual bungalows and the Sands had small du-plex suites. The en-tertainers knew to eat their meals in their rooms because they were not permitted in the restaurants or the casinos.

Entertainers began to appear all over the city. Arthur Simpkins, known as the golden-voiced tenor, was at the Last Frontier and Ruth Daye was on that same bill.

The Mills Brothers at the Nevada Biltmore in 1946. Las Vegas News Bureau

The Delta Rhythm Boys at the El Rancho in 1946. Las Vegas News Bureau

Nevada Biltmore Hotel in 1947. Las Vegas News Bureau

Langston Nobel and his orchestra also appeared at the hotel and the Mills Brothers played the Nevada Biltmore. Nick Lucas and the Nicholas Brothers played the El Rancho and Sister Rosetta Thorpe and Madam Marie Knight performed a gospel show at the War Memorial Building.

The Four Seasons once performed with Bing Crosby. They changed their name to the Charioteers and performed for an entire month at the Last Frontier. The Will Mastin Trio continued to play at the El Rancho Vegas, the Delta River Boys were at the Biltmore, and the Red Caps were at the Last Frontier.

As 1947 reached the halfway mark, changes became more and more noticeable. The black entertainers became the driving force behind the gambling business. A perfect match was made and the trade papers around town began to share the news. Las Vegas was starting to become a show town.

Aunt Mac said that even though black entertainers were partially responsible for bringing in millions to the city, they were being paid only a small portion of what the hotels were grossing.

Chapter

The Toast of the Town

*"At least we got a taste of integration,
even if it only lasted two weeks."*

The 1950s marked the beginning of the major hotel expansions in
Las Vegas. The marquees along Fremont Street and on the Strip
proclaimed black entertainment. There were eleven new hotels
and eight of them were on the Strip. As more hotels opened, the
competition for entertainment grew.

The new acts that headlined downtown and the Strip were
mostly blacks. The Golden Gate Quartet played the Last Frontier,
Brother Burns the Club Bingo, the Ink Spots the Thunderbird,
Arthur Duncan the Bingo, the Four Knights the El Cortez and
the Treniers played the Riviera.

The New Frontier had Carmen Miranda and the Mary Kay
Trio, the Sands headlined the Delta Rhythm Boys and Freddie
Bell, and Louie Prima and Keeley Smith were at the Sahara along
with Billy Ward and the Dominoes.

The El Cortez published an entertainment guide called
Fabulous Las Vegas. It showcased all the performers in town and
made sure everybody's act was a "must see." The publication not
only provided information about who, what and where the entertainment in town was appearing, it gave visitors a quick glimpse
of Las Vegas as a city.

☙ ❧

The Golden Quartet. Geran Family Collection

The segregation wall appeared to be slowly coming down. The residents on the Westside began to develop more businesses and casinos, and for the first time a white-owned hotel opened its doors to black patrons.

The Shamrock Hotel had been open a few years. It was located at Main and Bonanza, which was just a few blocks from the Westside.

The lounge had a bar and a jukebox. The blacks met there on weekends and enjoyed having the option of going to a place that was not far from their front yards.

The blacks didn't experience any signs of racism from the white employees or guests and every once in a while the manager would visit the lounge to introduce himself and to see if things were going okay. And they were until one night someone decided to jump in the pool.

Aunt mac said that a guy named Paps had one too many shots of whiskey. He started talking loud and removing his clothes. He yelled, "Damn, it's hot in here." Everyone in the place started to get nervous.

A few of the guys tried putting his jacket back on, but he grabbed it and threw it on the floor. With only his red boxers on, Paps ran out the door toward the pool. Then there was a splash.

Afraid he might drown, everyone ran to his rescue. Paps had jumped in the middle of the pool and started swimming on his back. And just like everyone suspected, the manager came out and immediately called security. Aunt Mac said, "At least we got a taste of integration, even if it only lasted for two weeks."

The Westside added a few new clubs. They were the El Rio, the Louisiana Club, the New Town Tavern and the Key Club. The owners were black businessmen.

The Louisiana and the El Rio were considered casual places. Most of their customers were guys who stopped by after work with their work clothes still on.

The New Town Tavern was adjacent to the Cotton Club. The owner was a black man named Earl Turman. It began to attract a lot of the entertainers. Its style and elegance were similar to the Cotton Club.

It was nothing to walk into the New Town Tavern and see Sonny Liston (at that time an up-and-coming boxer), Chubby Checker, Cab Calloway, Nat King Cole or Sammy Davis Jr. shooting craps or sitting at the bar mixing and mingling with the other patrons. It was just a matter of time before Nat sat down at the piano and Sammy found a microphone for at least an hour or two.

Sony Liston in front of a liquor store on Jackson and D Streets.
Special Collections, UNLV Library

Front of the New Town Tavern. Special Collections, UNLV Library

The Treniers. Geran Family Collection

Aunt Mac thought that Cab Calloway was a very bold man. One day he decided to visit the Jerry's Nugget and ignore the no-coloreds-allowed rule. Because he had a fair complexion and straight hair, they ignored his race. After a few sessions at the craps table, one of the floor bosses noticed how Calloway said the word "motherfuck" every time he would lose. The floor boss finally got the nerve to walk over and soon realized it was Cab Calloway. He gave Cab his money back and politely had him escorted out the door.

Across the street from the New Town Tavern was Smokey's Pool Hall, owned by Smokey Bowels, and next to the Hall was the Shadey Rest, which was a club for teenagers. It served soda pop and was known for having the latest hits on its jukebox.

Redd Foxx on stage on the Strip.
Las Vegas News Bureau

Most of these clubs were located on or near Jackson Street. The Westside's "Black Strip" began to emerge into adulthood.

The Key Club was the idea of a group of guys who wanted to create their own hangout. The membership was $3 a month and in order to enter the club, you had to have a key, which was given only to members.

The members were all black men, but Aunt Mac said there were a few women who were an exception to the rule. Located inside was a small restaurant and bar. The establishment of this club was said to have assisted in building pride

Comedian Slappy White. Geran Family Collection

Prince Spencer. Geran Family Collection

and dignity among the men. It was important for them to have a place of their own.

Two doors down from the Key Club was Sportsman Barbershop. Johnus, the barber and Hazel's husband, had star clients that included comedian and actor Redd Foxx (*Sanford & Son*), comedian Slappy White and George Kirby. Others included drummer, Calvin "Eagle Eye" Shields, and Redd's friend and head-line opener, Prince Spencer. The Mills Brothers, The Treniers and The Ink Spots were regulars, and Joe Louis, Sonny Liston and

Comedian George Kirby on horse. Geran Family Collection

Actor Greg Morris. Geran Family Collection

Drummer Calvin "Eagle Eye" Shields, whose list of clients included such greats as: Tiny Bradshaw, Della Reese and Redd Fox. Geran Family Collection

Sugar Ray Robinson were known to drop by for a lining when they were in town. Actor Greg Morris (*Mission: Impossible*) was also a regular.

The young guys looked at Johnus as a father figure. The ones who had unknown or distant fathers instantly attached themselves to him. Not only did they come for a haircut and shave, they came to talk and receive his advice on how to live and survive. Johnus was known in the community for his grandfatherly storytelling.

Johnus had spent a few months in jail and went only as far as the eighth grade. But he had staying power and a keen sense of how to survive, and most of his customers were starving for it.

Sportsman was a popular barbershop not because it was near the clubs, but because of its proximity to a new soul food restaurant called Mom's Kitchen. It was located a few doors down and was on the same side of the street as the shop. The restaurant was named after the owner's wife's nickname, Mom.

Mom's Kitchen had half a dozen large leather booths, three on each side, eight counter chairs and lots of standing room for the take-out customers. During the summertime, Mom had one large fan circulating in the middle of the ceiling. Aunt Mac believed it generated heat rather than the cool air that was expected.

The kitchen was in the front area of the room and every time a waiter picked up an order, wooden doors opened, allowing a blast of heat from the kitchen to rush into the restaurant.

When it was 100-plus degrees outside, Mom's Kitchen was like a sweatshop, but that didn't stop the crowd from coming. Sometimes it was so hot, Aunt Mac would pay a kid to walk in and pick up her order. She didn't want the curls in her hair to fall.

Mom was an excellent cook. She was known to cook the kind of food that stuck to your ribs for three days.

One day, Aunt Mac saw a guy pouring Tabasco on his ox tails. It was funny watching him prepare to eat and sweat. He held a fork in one hand and a damp towel in the other. One was for eating and the other was for keeping the sweat from dripping into his food. That's how delicious her food tasted.

Johnus became like a son to Mom and her husband, Mr. Walker. Every day, he would call to see if things were going okay or if they needed anything. And if he didn't see Mr. Walker's car parked out front, he would close his shop for a minute and walk down. He knew a lot of bad actors hung around the restaurant and she needed extra protection.

Everybody knew Johnus carried a gun just in case someone tried to rob him, and that he was so fond of Mom and Walker, he would defend them as well.

Mr. Walker was a tall, skinny man who was quiet and calm. He was known as a man of few words. Aunt Mac couldn't imagine him hurting anyone, even in self-defense.

One morning, around six a.m., the cook hadn't shown up for work yet. Mom continued to work way beyond her usual hours in the kitchen, while Mr. Walker took the orders and watched the cash register. The restaurant was empty and the streets were quiet.

A man walked in still dressed in the previous night's evening attire. He was high on heroin mixed with a few pints of whiskey. Mom said he looked like he was coming down for a crash landing.

The man sat at the counter and Mr. Walker politely handed him a menu. Without even looking at it, he threw it back and screamed at the top of his lungs, "I already know what I want. Give me some collards with hot water cornbread and hurry the fuck up!" Mr. Walker, still calm and cool as usual, nodded and wrote down the items on his little white pad.

After he gave the order to Mom, he sat a glass of water in front of the man on the counter. "Did I ask for this?" the man said angrily. Mr. Walker remained quiet.

Ten minutes later, the man began to complain about the heat. Mom rang the bell and said "Order up." Mr. Walker walked over and placed the plate in front of the customer. Suddenly the man yelled, "These ain't no collards, these are greens!" He threw the plate at the wall and grabbed Mr. Walker by the collar. Mr. Walker continued to remain silent.

Mom ran out and Mr. Walker told her to go back inside the kitchen. Mr. Walker continued to struggle with the guy, while Mom went to the phone and called Johnus.

Because he lived only a few blocks away, in less than five minutes he was at the restaurant. When Johnus arrived, he told Mr. Walker to give him the gun that was in the back of his pants. Without hesitating, Mr. Walker surrendered the small handgun.

The guy sobered when he saw the gun and fled the scene. Mr. Walker just stood there with his shirt torn down the front. Johnus said he looked like a scared little puppy.

Mom took extra precaution and contacted the police. Two minutes after the call, two white officers arrived. They asked if things were okay and said that they didn't want anything happening to their favorite spot to eat. They handed Mom a card that had the direct number to call in case of an emergency.

Around that time, the police department finally hired a few black men to be on the force. They were not able to arrest a white man. They could only hold him until a white cop came. Aunt Mac said, "The black cops were more like baby sitters than police officers."

In 1955, a new hotel called the Moulin Rouge was granted its license to open. It became the first integrated hotel-casino in Las Vegas and was the first modern hotel on the Westside.

The former heavyweight boxer Joe Louis was the host and official greeter at the hotel. It was said that he was placed in that position so the hotel could attract wealthy blacks. He supposedly had two percent in stock and was the only black to have any form of ownership. The owners of the Moulin Rouge were a group of private investors.

The blacks in Las Vegas felt the Moulin Rouge was their first major accomplishment in Las Vegas and the Westside's showplace. It was the first beacon of freedom the black residents had experienced.

Following its opening, black entertainers no longer had to pay the high rent to stay in private homes. The Moulin Rouge cost an estimated $6.9 million. It had over 200 rooms and created an aura that made the entertainers feel proud.

Chandeliers hung from lavender ceilings and each table was softly lit with lamps, creating a very intimate atmosphere. Aunt Mac said that some of the people began to call it the "jewel of the desert."

It was as plush as any hotel on the Strip and proved that a mixed-race crowd could enjoy themselves. It offered all the gaming, entertainment and comfort that could be found anywhere. It featured a chorus line of gorgeous black girls, and the bands contracted to play were the "Great" Benny Carter and Lionel Hampton and his twelve-piece orchestra. Every once in while Sammy Davis Jr. would do a solo on the drums.

When Sammy described the Westside as "Tobacco Road," he saw that the streets were unpaved and a large number of homes didn't have sanitary facilities. This is why the people felt the Moulin Rouge was God-sent and some even said the opening of the Rouge placed Las Vegas on the map for civil rights development in the nation.

The Moulin Rouge became a meeting place for entertainers after their second show. The first shows on the Strip began at eight p.m. and included dinner. At the midnight show, a two-drink minimum was offered. The Moulin Rouge had the same schedule except for the third show, which was added by popular demand.

The last show started at two a.m. and it was pure entertainment. That's when stars like Harry Belafonte, Louis Armstrong, Lena Horne, Frank Sinatra, The Treniers, Dean Martin, Sammy

The Moulin Rouge. Special Collections, UNLV Library

Lionel Hampton at the Moulin Rouge. Special Collections, UNLV Library

Black showgirls at the Moulin Rouge. Special Collections, UNLV Library

Davis Jr., Tallulah Bankhead, Gregory Peck, Dorothy Lamour, Bob Hope and Milton Berle would come out to see the black revue.

Sometimes the guest entertainers would perform their stage acts just for the fun of it and some came to kick up their heels and join in on the late-late-night jam sessions. The original Platters and Gregory Hines and his brother Maurice, known as The Hines Kids, got their start at the Moulin Rouge.

There were always white limousines parked out front and an array of photographers flashing their cameras inside and outside the place. The Moulin Rouge was a club filled with surprises. Aunt mac said you never knew who to expect.

Trying to leave the Rouge before five in the morning was always a challenge for Aunt Mac. The party went into second gear around two a.m., and there was so much energy in the room that it was hard to walk out the door. On many occasions, she and her cousins got into trouble with their husbands over their all-night outings.

The Strip and downtown hotel owners were beginning to resent the competition. Most of the hotels the entertainers performed in were practically empty by two a.m. Because the entertainers and showgirls started to rush over to the Rouge after work, it began to take a toll on the other hotels' revenue. A clause was established that required the entertainers to remain on the premises for a certain amount of time after their last show.

Most of the black people who came to visit Las Vegas didn't know the city was segregated until after they arrived. It was never publicized. The image the black newcomers had was that it was a place to go if you wanted to get away from it all.

Before the Moulin Rouge opened, those who found out about the prejudices that hid beyond the glimmering lights would simply turn around and go home. They felt that since they traveled all these miles and were denied access to the areas in town they came to see, there really wasn't any reason to stay.

In October, seven months after its grand opening, the Moulin Rouge closed its doors. The owners said it was because of mismanagement and a lack of funds. But even if this was true, the blacks in Las Vegas knew there was a long list of interested buyers who desperately wanted to purchase the hotel.

Some say the doors closed because of skimming or that it was planned to fail by rival hotel owners, but Aunt Mac said they were both lies. The truth, she said, was the Moulin Rouge was too competitive for the segregated Strip and downtown hotels and they really did not anticipate it being so successful in such a short time.

&>∾

As black entertainers became major attractions, the hotels on the Strip began to lift their strict racial rules a little. Louis Armstrong and Eartha Kitt were able to sleep and eat in the hotels where they played as long as they stayed out of management's way and didn't invite their friends and relatives to the shows.

In 1954, Eartha Kitt headlined at the El Rancho Vegas. In her autobiography, *Thursday's Child*, she describes the experience:

> On April 7, 1954, I opened at the El Rancho Vegas in Las Vegas, Nevada. I remember when I got off the plane in the desert, a member of the hotel staff was there to meet me with my secretary, who had gone ahead to make preparations. Driving from the airport to the highway, I saw a sign advertising the star that was to appear at the El Rancho. Letters taller than I spelled a name that I could not make a complete identification with — EARTHA KITT.
>
> When we reached the hotel, a sign on each side of the road said the same thing. Someone had something

Actress-singer Eartha Kitt signing ann autograph for a fan at the El Rancho. Special Collections, UNLV Library

Actress-singer Eartha Kitt sitting on a conga drum. Las Vegas News Bureau

to do with me becoming a headliner. I was taken to my cabin of luxury that was just like a regular little house, everything included. A bottle of champagne waited in a bucket. Flowers scented my room. I felt strange and alone, but wanted.

In her first show at the Last Frontier, Josephine Baker noticed there were no blacks in the audience. Between shows, she asked what was the hotel's policy regarding negroes entering the showroom. She was told that coloreds were not allowed. Josephine politely said that if they did not admit negroes in for the second show, she was going to walk off the stage.

When the black workers in the hotel discovered what her demand was, everyone stood near the showroom to witness what the result would be. When the curtain was raised, Josephine paused

Josephine Baker sitting in chair. Special Collections, Oakland Library

and looked in the audience. In the front row, there was a black couple sitting at a table. The man was dressed in a tuxedo and the woman was in a lovely evening gown. Aunt Mac said later they discovered that the manager of the showroom pulled a porter and a maid off their shifts and dressed them in formal attire.

It was a hot summer day and Josephine decided to take a dip in the pool. Immediately after she left the area, the white guests demanded that it be drained. Not only did they have it drained, it was also cleaned. Even though she honored her contract and the pool incident wasn't called to her attention, Josephine Baker never returned to Las Vegas.

Although the rule "you can sometimes stay but never play" was very humiliating to the entertainers, sometimes there was a bit of humor involved.

Black singer Herb Jeffries was told when he arrived that his room would be among the white guests but his piano accompanist, Dick Hazzard, would have to stay in the special negro quarters. "If he does, I do," Jeffries said. Minutes later, Herb introduced Dick to the owner of the hotel. He was shocked when he saw that Dick was a white man

∂∞∾

Nat King Cole was one of the premier crooners at that time. Everywhere he played he sold out. In 1956, he came to Las Vegas and was offered $4,500 a week to play at the Thunderbird Hotel.

When Nat's road manager, Mort Ruby, a white man, was given a suite at the hotel free of charge during their engagement, it meant he would have to find somewhere for Nat to stay.

Mort caught a cab and went looking for a place for Nat to stay. He went door-to-door and nothing was available until he stumbled across the filthiest, dirtiest motel he had ever seen that claimed to have one room left. When the owner told Mort the charge would be $15 a day, he couldn't believe it.

Aunt Mac said Nat used to rent a room at Mrs. Simpson's house on the Westside. Simpson said Nat felt honored to make a decent living and proud to earn so much money. Money was the only reason he tolerated the mistreatment by the hotels.

One day when Mrs. Simpson was cleaning Nat's room, she looked over in the corner and saw a suitcase filled with nothing but conk and grease. She said he was a man who cared a great deal about the appearance of his hair.

On top of a dresser was a folded check stub. She looked at it and all she could see were four black numbers typed in the amount area. She didn't open it because she was afraid he would notice it had been tampered with. Nat was one of her best customers and she couldn't afford to lose his business.

Aunt Mac said Mrs. Simpson was the type of woman who was prim and proper during the day, but at night she could be found on Mary Nettles' porch sipping gin.

Nat King Cole could not go into the casino or anywhere else in the hotel except in a sitting area adjoining the kitchen's entrance. After tolerating so many unjust incidents, Nat vowed to never play Las Vegas again unless conditions changed.

Two years after Nat made his stand, Beldon Katleman, one of the few sole owners of a hotel on the Strip, the El Rancho, wanted to book the Will Mastin Trio and Carlos Gastel. But Will politely told him that the only way they would appear at his hotel was if he would use his connections the next time Nat and the boys came to town.

Nat King Cole sitting at piano. Las Vegas News Bureau

Will wanted Beldon to make sure Nat could live, eat, gamble, drink or whatever he and his guys wanted to do at the El Rancho without any prejudice shown against them. Beldon agreed and the next time Nat performed in Las Vegas, he was given the "red carpet" treatment. Not only did Will take a stand for Nat, so did Frank Sinatra.

While headlining at the Sands Hotel, Frank Sinatra noticed on numerous occasions that Nat King Cole would eat dinner in his dressing room. Finally Sinatra asked his valet, a black man named George Jacobs, what was the reason behind that. George answered, "I don't know, maybe he like eating in the nude or something." Then, with a straight face, George told him that coloreds weren't allowed in the dining room. This really pissed Sinatra off because he thought the world of Nat. Sinatra immediately told the maitre' d's and waitresses that if that ever happened again, everyone would be fired. The next night he told Nat to meet him in the Garden Room for dinner.

Lena Horne, Eartha Kitt, Sammy Davis Jr., Louis Armstrong and the few others who were allowed to stay, but not play, in the hotels where they performed started a movement toward dissolving segregation. When the owner of a hotel gave Nat King Cole carte blanche, it was just a matter of time before the wall of racism would come tumbling down for everyone.

☙ ❧

When Harry Belafonte performed in the showroom at the Sands Hotel, he was allowed to stay on the premises but not play. One day after his second show, around three a.m., Harry decided to take a seat at the blackjack table for a couple of rounds of chance, regardless of what the understood rule was for blacks. The dealer just stood there not knowing what to do. He then took a few steps back. The person in the eye-in-the-sky (surveillance camera room) gave a message to the floorman and that message was given to the dealer. Harry received the green light.

Harry Belafonte. Special Collections, Oakland Library

Suddenly a crowd began to gather around the table. Some gambled and some just stared at the famous calypso singer. When the guests who were upstairs sleeping heard that Harry Belafonte was in the casino gambling, they immediately came down in their pajamas to get a quick peek for themselves.

Aunt Mac's friend Porter was a janitor at the New Frontier Hotel when Sammy Davis Jr. performed there. In 1956, Sammy had risen to stardom and he was in great demand. When he opened in the Venus Room, the occasion was sensational in more ways than one. Porter said no one could believe Sammy had his grandmother, stepmother and sister sitting in the front row of the showroom. Porter said they enjoyed the entire show.

Because there was no force or demand made, Sammy Davis Jr. is considered by the blacks in Las Vegas to be the first entertainer to break the color barrier in the showrooms.

Chapter

Having Our Say
"I tell you, us colored folks just can't seem to win in Las Vegas."

n the 1950s, the city was undergoing major changes. On April 28, 1954, the Federal Bureau of Investigation (FBI) raided the popular Roxie's Resort brothel (five dollars for fifteen minutes). The charges against the owners, Eddie and Roxie Clippinger, were based on the Mann Act, which prohibited transporting girls across state lines for immoral purposes. The case went to trial in a Los Angeles federal court.

When Roxie's closed its doors, Maxine's opened. Maxine's was a club for lesbians and was located at the corner of Charleston and Nellis. It was referred to as an offbeat tavern. The Tail O' the Pup was another spot where "the girls" were known to hang out.

Aunt Mac's cousin, Erwin, finally made the difficult decision to leave Binion's Horseshoe Hotel to work for the Alstate Coin Machine Company Inc., a slot machine repair company. He said he loved his job because it allowed him the opportunity to answer calls at the client's place of business.

Erwin's territory was Southern Nevada and his clients included Roxie's, Maxine's and Tail O' the Pup. Every week he received a call concerning their poker and slot machines. Erwin said Roxie's was a plush brothel but what really made it popular was that it was the only place in town that had a big-screen television.

Erwin "Brother" Wilburn leaning on slot machine. Geran Family Collection

Erwin said the regulars in the lesbian clubs who were popular around town were singers Keely Smith and Mary Kaye, and strippers Candy Barr and Evalyn Scott.

He said the lesbian prostitutes were known to play the high-rollers for all they could get and then devote their playtime to women.

৵৽

Lee Birda left the El Rancho Vegas and went to work as a powder room attendant at the New Frontier Hotel. Aunt Mac said Lee Birda was known as Momma Lee. The white cocktail waitresses were crazy about her and they valued their relationship. On the first day they met Lee, most of them immediately adopted her as their Momma.

Lee Birda Rose sitting on couch with cocktail waitresses. Rose Family Collection

The regulars who frequented the powder room included hookers, co-workers and tourists. But to Lee Birda, it didn't matter what they did for a living or what color they were, she would still be their Momma if they wanted her to. Aunt Mac said that whenever they needed a shoulder to cry on, Lee Birda held up many heads that tried to fall down.

ॐॐ

The black club owners of the El Rio, El Morocco, Brown Derby, Cotton Club, New Town Tavern and Louisiana Club on the Westside began to sell their shares in the casino parts of their businesses. They were having more and more trouble paying their customers whenever a large sum was won. They either had to bring in a partner or take a chance on losing it all.

Aunt Mac said sometimes the owners would go to the nearest pawnshop in the middle of the night to sell a ring or watch because they didn't have enough money to pay winners. Most of

Fat Calvin at the El Morrocco Club craps table. Special Collections, UNLV Library

them didn't have the experience of running a casino, but they did have a knack for managing a bar.

Their new partners often were Chinese businessmen. A man named Lee ran the keno at the New Town Tavern and the Louisiana Club. He also ran the craps game and even dealt cards. Gene, who the blacks called Jeno, owned and leased the gaming section at the El Rio and a white man was in charge of the bar. Zee Louie was another Chinese investor who gained interest in several of the clubs. He was known as "the big man" on the Westside.

Even though the 1950s brought a lot of positive changes for blacks in Las Vegas, especially the entertainers, a black-owned magazine called *Ebony* contradicted those facts.

In March 1954, an article titled "Negroes Can't Win in Las Vegas" was written by James Goodrich. Mr. Goodrich described the blacks in Las Vegas as nothing but sellouts. It was a humiliating article.

Aunt Mac said when the issue hit the newsstands, an atomic bomb went off on the Westside. After she read the first page, she

Chinese businessman Lee at craps table. Special Collections, UNLV Library

Negro gamblers crowd around dice table at Cotton Club. Silver dollars are vogue in Las Vegas, are easier for gamblers to handle than paper money. Betting maximum at most clubs is $500. A $100 win in silver dollars is almost too heavy to carry. Las Vegas has four Negro cops on local police force. They patrol all areas of the city.

NEGROES CAN'T WIN IN LAS VEGAS

Ebony Magazine *Article: "Negroes Can't Win In Las Vegas." Oakland Library*

immediately called her mama to hear what the folks back home thought about it. Her mama said that she as well as everyone else was shocked. They were under the assumption that the blacks in Las Vegas were living the "good life." Aunt Mac's last words to her mama before hanging up the phone were, "I tell you, us colored folks just can't seem to win in Las Vegas."

Surprisingly, Goodrich's started off with good intentions. He called the Sahara Hotel and asked if he could interview a negro movie star who was appearing in their showroom. They agreed and Goodrich immediately made plans to visit Las Vegas for the first time.

He arrived at the airport and stood on the curb waiting for a cab. There were two cab companies at the time, Checker and Lucky 7-11, and blacks were not able to use their services, especially to and from the Westside.

After ten cabs passed without stopping, he knew it was because of the color of his skin. He realized his chance of catching a cab was as good as hitting a jackpot. He called the Sahara and they said they would send a car for him. They thought he knew what the rules were for blacks in Las Vegas.

On the way to the hotel, the white hotel executive told him about the "facts of life" for blacks in Vegas. The news upset Goodrich even more than the four-hour wait at the airport.

By the end of the day, Goodrich was well aware what the rules were. From the balcony he caught the show and afterward, he interviewed the negro star in her cabin.

A few hours before his plane was due to depart, Goodrich decided to visit the Westside. He walked up and down Jackson Street, looking inside some of the businesses and casinos. He then asked one of the guys in a club to give him a ride to the airport. He paid a generous amount for the ten-minute ride.

Aunt Mac said a few of the residents saw him around town, but no one actually talked to him. After being in Las Vegas for one day, Mr. Goodrich left. Four months after his departure, his article was published and it thoroughly explained black life in Las Vegas. And at that time, Las Vegas was labeled as being the *Best City of Them All.*

The subtitle of the article was "Nevada Gambling Town Has More Racial Barriers Than Any Other Place Outside of Dixie." A section read:

A Negro celebrity, concluding a stopover in Las Vegas recently, sized up the Nevada boom town this way: "It's like some place in Mississippi – downright prejudiced and really rough on colored people. It's worse than any place in Mississippi!"

Aunt Mac added, "I can't say that it was worse but it was sure damn close."

Goodrich continued:

Negroes themselves could be a great deal to blame for their lowly position in the town. Some locals think they are, and claim it is due to their interaction. The record shows that Negroes of Las Vegas have never been very active in civic matters. While representing as much as 10 per cent of the town's population, they still exert no pressure on the city government. They have never demonstrated they could band together in civil rights matters and generally seem to be "don't carish" about issues directly concerning them. Close observers think their complacency can be explained away by the fact that many of them are illiterates only recently migrated West from the rural South.

Just about every black person in the United States had that issue in his or her home. This flustered the blacks in Las Vegas. Now everybody knew what was really going on. A bitter taste began to develop for the city they were starting to call home.

Aunt Mac said that although the article painted a horrific picture of the black experience in Las Vegas, it was the spark they needed to move them out of their comfort zones.

The local NAACP president, Dr. James B. McMillan a dentist, along with assistance from the national branch, began to hold meetings in the town hall and in some of the churches. Aunt Mac said that before each meeting, someone would lead them in prayer.

One time, immediately after everyone said "Amen," a man stood up and yelled, "I'm mad as hell and I'm not taking this anymore." The crowd cheered him on. He couldn't have said it better.

For the NAACP president and board members and the residents, the days turned into years of meeting, and countless rejections from the powers that be. The blacks began to empower themselves to become stronger politically.

McMillan determined that threats were not going to be enough, that they needed certain politicians involved in their mission. Since the NAACP was not allowed to favor politicians, he and a friend and an executive board member, Dr. Charles West, decided to form the Nevada Voters League in 1957.

The League was like a sister organization to the NAACP and was located within the branch's walls. Its purpose was to make sure the members and residents were registered to vote. To blacks in those days, a vote meant they counted and that they had a say in things. Aunt Mac said, "It meant you had power."

Aunt Mac decided to volunteer a few hours a day at the NAACP office. It didn't matter what chores were assigned to her,

The life members of the NAACP. Las Vegas Sun Newspaper

she simply wanted to feel like she was part of the team of individuals who were trying to make a difference. She made sure her friends were registered and actively involved as well.

Her duties included answering phones, licking stamps and making sure the past and present members were registered voters. She was also responsible for taking the names of those who wanted to become NAACP Life Members.

A man named Oran Gragson was running for mayor and he promised he would be for all people. Aunt Mac trusted Gragson and felt he was sincere. She hinted to all of the registered voters to mark an "x" for Gragson.

Oran Gragson won the election. Soon after he was sworn in as the mayor of Las Vegas, Oran insisted blacks be hired for municipal jobs, and so they were. The fact that Mayor Gragson kept his word and a black man received assistance from the majority of white politicians in the Nevada Legislature seemed to hold promise that a political change for the better was around the corner.

Although no major civil rights bills were passed in the Nevada Legislature in the 1950s, in 1959, McMillan was the force behind a bill that permitted interracial marriage in the state.

&⤳

In 1960, meetings continued between local officers of the NAACP, Governor Grant Sawyer, Mayor Oran Gragson, county commissioners, law enforcement officials and the gaming industry concerning the removal of the color barrier.

Hank Greenspun, owner of the *Las Vegas Sun* newspaper, was the mediator. Greenspun was the voice of the black people and he was very knowledgeable about the city's rules and regulations as well as its past and present state from a political standpoint. His advice helped to steer the meetings in the direction the NAACP and the residents wanted it to go.

There were two newspapers, the *Las Vegas Sun* and *Las Vegas Review-Journal*. At the time, the *Sun* wrote a great deal more about blacks than the *R-J*. The *R-J* rarely printed extensive articles that concerned blacks, whether it was good news or bad.

For years, McMillan and Greenspun only managed to accomplish countless and meaningless talks. Then a correspondence letter from the national office was sent to all of the presidents of the NAACP branches calling for them to organize and do away with unjust treatments in their cities.

The letter stated, "All branches should do everything possible to eliminate all visages of discriminations in its regions." After McMillan read this, he felt his first order of business should be the hotel-casinos.

McMillan realized that not only did he have the national NAACP on his side, but all the other branches were on the same page as well. He was convinced that to have that many blacks fighting for the same cause at the same time meant that he had the power to go after the gaming industry.

After McMillan met with his executive board about the matter, a decision was made to write a letter to Mayor Gragson to inform him that they had received instructions from national to take action against segregation in their community. He stated that their number one problem was with the hotel-casinos. He gave Gragson thirty days to respond to the idea of dissolving segregation.

McMillan wanted the letter to stir things up, but at first it didn't. A reporter named Alan Jarlson for the *Sun* phoned and said he saw the letter in the mayor's office and asked if he could use it as a basis to begin a movement. McMillan agreed.

After the NAACP letter was published, McMillan didn't receive one call from anyone with influence stating that the end of segregation was even being discussed. But when Greenspun began to write daily about civil rights in his "Where I Stand" column, which was printed on the front page of his newspaper, letters and phone calls flooded his office.

A national radio show that was broadcast from the Fremont Hotel downtown called and said they were going to air this matter on their show. McMillan added that there was a thirty-day deadline or a march of 300 demonstrators on the Las Vegas Strip would take place.

When the world heard about the NAACP's plan to protest, Aunt Mac said, "Everything and everyone went crazy." Other radio and television stations began to cover the story. The tourists could not believe that the Entertainment Capital of the World was going to allow something like this to happen.

The pressure was building and the thirty-day deadline was getting closer. The ministers began to get nervous. They suggested that McMillan cancel the march. They were worried that a crazed person might try to burn down the Westside.

Mayor Gragson and business leader Reed Whipple tried to convince McMillan to call off the march. The mayor promised that the city would hire more blacks and Reed Whipple, the president of First National Bank, agreed that he would start granting small business and home loans to blacks.

Gragson and Whipple said that they did not have the power or the influence to end segregation in the hotel-casinos.

McMillan decided to continue focusing on the gaming industry, which was represented by the Las Vegas Resort Association. He had two weeks left until the deadline.

McMillan was starting to get nervous and frustrated. There were pep rallies at the local churches to keep the dream alive, but still the thought of not being able to pull this off began to weigh heavily on his mind. He wondered if he was going to have to leave town.

McMillan received phone threats at his home. A group of men had to escort him everywhere he went and stay overnight to make sure no one tried to burn down his home with a bomb or drive-by shooting. The threats on his life began to increase by the hour.

Oscar Crozier, the former owner of the El Morocco, called McMillan and said he would like to meet with him. Oscar had close ties with some of the underworld figures. He said that investors in the major hotels had flown to Las Vegas for a meeting concerning the NAACP's demands. He was told to pass a message to McMillan, that he should be careful or he might find himself floating face down in Lake Mead.

McMillan told Crozier they were not going to get off that easy. He wasn't a gambler and he wasn't trying to cut into their business. All he was trying to do was make Las Vegas into a cosmopolitan city.

Later that evening, Crozier called and said the guys said no and for him to be cool. McMillan said that he was going to continue with his plans.

Three days before the deadline, Crozier called again but this time his tone was different. He said the casino guys had decided to agree to the NAACP's terms. They were going to allow blacks to play and stay in the hotels and he could announce that there would be no more discrimination in the hotels and casinos.

The next day, McMillan and Greenspun called a meeting at the Moulin Rouge and announced that segregation would end in the hotels and casinos. The day was March 26, 1960, and the time recorded was six p.m.

Although the Moulin Rouge was not operating as a hotel or casino, the doors were still open for meetings and special gatherings. Aunt Mac said McMillan chose the Moulin Rouge because a lot of good memories continued to linger there. It was where he married his first wife, and present at the wedding were Sammy Davis Jr. and Frank Sinatra.

Just hours before the meeting took place, Greenspun had the news printed on the front page so that during the meeting the papers would already be on the stands. However, the minute the papers hit the stands, it sold. The demand was so incredible that Greenspun had to print more.

On that day, the *Sun* published two newspapers with different headlines on the front page. The captions read "Vegas Color

March 26, 1960 front page reads, "Vegas Color Barrier Lifted After Parley." Las Vegas Sun

Barrier Lifted After Parley" and "Businesses In Vegas Lift Color Barrier."

McMillan stated in one of the newspapers, "We are happy we didn't have to resort to this type of action." He went on to say, "We believe this is a red-letter day in Las Vegas."

McMillan wanted to make sure the hotels and casinos were aware that discrimination against their black patrons was no longer allowed, that integration was the new "understood law."

To make sure it was enforced, he decided to form groups of ten made up of NAACP members and test the hotels. The instructions were to visit the assigned casino to see if any discriminatory treatment was displayed. If so, they were to report back immediately to the office.

Each group had the same experience: They were allowed to gamble among the white patrons. They were granted access to the front door and were welcomed at the tables in all of the casinos except at two, Binion's Horseshoe and Sal Sagev (Las Vegas spelled backward).

McMillan felt that maybe it would be best for him to tackle these two. His plan for the owner of Sal Sagev, Abe Miller, was to take a paraplegic black man named Alan Sharp with him so he could gain entry. He was confident Abe wouldn't have the heart to deny a man in a wheelchair, but he was wrong.

McMillan took along a board member and as soon as they entered the door, the security guard threw all three of them out, including the wheelchair. Aunt Mac said the gossip around town was that Abe Miller's wife had just eloped with a black man and he was extremely upset about it. To have a black man in his casino was the last thing he wanted to see.

When McMillan called Benny Binion and asked if he would call a truce, Binion said nobody was going to him how to operate his hotel. He would allow access to blacks when the time was right for him.

Aunt Mac said even though Binion named one of his horses Nigger, that didn't mean he was a racist hotel owner. He had been known to practice integration from time to time. He simply catered to his needs accordingly.

McMillan knew Gold Dollar was Binion's bodyguard and they didn't want to upset the 300-pound guy in any way. Aunt Mac said McMillan was not only afraid physically, he was also afraid of losing him as a client. McMillan was the mastermind behind Dollar's gold teeth.

McMillan said that after all the talks and meetings with the state's top politicians, it was really the guys from the underworld who ended segregation in the hotel and gaming industry.

He said around that time, twelve million tourists had spent an estimated $3 billion in the casinos and the mob had invested about $250 million and they were not going to let anyone take that away from them. McMillan concluded by saying, "There is no doubt about it, Las Vegas belongs to the mob."

Chapter

The Beginning
"It's okay to party,
just know when it's over."

Soon after segregation was considered demolished by the hotel and gaming industry, the city agreed to make public accommodations and business establishments available to blacks. So now when a black person was seen downtown, on the Strip or on the white side of town, he didn't necessarily have to be associated with a broom, mop or dish cloth.

When the black entertainers agreed to assist the NAACP in their fight for justice, the enormous pressure from the tourists became unbearable for the hotels. The entertainers knew they were the hottest ticket in town and they felt deeply obligated to use this influence in order to create a change for the better. Some of them canceled engagements and some simply said no when asked to perform in the near future.

The hotel executives felt the losses from the showrooms would take a long time to regain, and the bruise the tourists received may never heal. They concluded that segregation was not worth it. The odds were definitely in the entertainers' favor. And Sammy Davis Jr. took full advantage of the demise of racism in the casinos and Frank Sinatra would make sure he did so.

It was public knowledge that Frank Sinatra was well connected with the Chicago mob. What he said went in Las Vegas. Whenever any headline act was sick or couldn't perform, he would send Sammy to fill in.

Frank Sinatra owned Reprise Records. He contracted groups such as the Treniers, the Mills Brothers, Count Basie, Duke Ellington, the Ink Spots and a trumpet player named Jonah Jones. He made sure that all his "guys" were working in Las Vegas around the clock.

Frank Sinatra, Sammy Davis Jr., Dean Martin, Joey Bishop and Peter Lawford decided to take their act from home to the stage at the Sands Hotel in Las Vegas.

In their spare time, the "guys" loved sitting around Sinatra's house in Palm Springs, California, drinking and shooting the breeze. They called the gathering a Summit, which, according to Webster's Dictionary, means "a conference between the heads of state." Sinatra was, of course, the Chairman of the Board. But according to Humphrey Bogart, the meeting consisted of nothing but a bunch of Beverly Hills rats. Surprisingly the "guys" loved their new title, and they began calling themselves the Rat Pack.

Sammy Davis Jr. seated with Dean Martin and Frank Sinatra. Las Vegas News Bureau

The Rat Pack (Peter, Frank, Dean, Sammy and Joey) on stage. Las Vegas News Bureau

After Dr. James McMillan's courageous crusade was accomplished, he decided to resign as the president of the NAACP Las Vegas branch. To his surprise, his resignation was accepted without any questions from his executive board.

For a long time, he wondered why his request wasn't refused or torn up on the spot. He was hurt, but remained committed to feeling that what he did was right and was done in the best possible way. He later found out that his board disagreed.

The board felt that his impatience could have resulted in a tragedy on the Westside. Aunt Mac said McMillan was the type of man who didn't believe in waiting. When he saw a project or a matter that needed addressing, he went after it as though his life depended on it. His approach may have offended those around him, but he didn't mean for it to.

From his jail cell, the late Dr. Martin Luther King wrote a letter to his clergymen who were against his behavior and urged patience. It read:

For years now I have heard the word "Wait!" It rings in the ear of every Negro with piercing familiarity. This "Wait" has almost always meant "Never." There comes a time when the cup of endurance runs over, and men are no longer willing to be plunged into the abyss of despair.

In other words, it's possible that if McMillan would have given the mayor three to six months as opposed to thirty days to respond, the conditions may have worsened for blacks in Las Vegas and that could have been the real tragedy.

⤞⤝

Aunt Mac said Hank Greenspun and his newspaper, the *Las Vegas Sun*, were a "saving grace" to the black people in Las Vegas. If it weren't for his continuous coverage of issues concerning blacks, it's no telling what the result may have been. His choice of topics and words definitely assisted in motivating blacks to push harder and want more. Not only were his articles entertaining, they were insightful as well.

On the front cover of the *Sun* on March 26, 1960, not only did Greenspun devote a full-page article as well as an entire additional page to the NAACP's efforts and victory, he also featured an article about the former NAACP president, Arthur McCants. It was located on the front as well.

In his column "Where I Stand," Greenspun stated the following about his long-time friend:

> There is a man who comes to the office quite often. He brings books for me to read, clippings from newspapers and just likes to sit and chat. The topic of conversation and the literature left with me all indicate the same theme; the greatest of his people. Whenever this man leaves, his parting words are "tell them about my people."

I sometimes wonder how many times Arthur McCants has told others to "tell them about my people." I wonder how many newspapers have been visited by Arthur McCants in his 82 years on earth, and how many editors have heard that same request, "tell them about my people."

I am going to accede to the wishes of this kindly, serene-featured, gentle person. My only regret is that I am not capable of doing justice to the assignment given me. Other men, far more able, must have turned a deaf ear, or Arthur would not find it necessary to continue the search for someone to listen to him.

Arthur McCants was the son of a slave who barely escaped slavery himself. He was born in Alabama in 1869 and became self-educated through his desire to read books. At 58 years old, Arthur McCants became the first NAACP president for Las Vegas' first branch in 1927.

ào ‹S›

In 1954, Aunt Mac joined an organization called the Order of the Eastern Star (O.E.S.). One year later, she attended the annual Grand Chapter meeting in Phoenix, Arizona, where the O.E.S. sisters were to meet their brothers, the Masons. The members came from all over the world.

After the last meeting took place, a formal dinner and dance was held. While talking with a friend at her table, a dark-complexioned man walked over, pulled her by the arm and began talking as though he had known her for years. After he introduced himself, in a matter of seconds, Aunt Mac knew he was "the one." "Oh what the hell, I guess seven is my lucky number." Aunt Mac said.

She used to say, "It's okay to party, just know when it's over." On June 10, 1956, Aunt Mac married her seventh husband, Wallace

Ferrell. She allowed him more than the average time of six months because in the beginning it was a platonic friendship. But soon it blossomed into a commitment. Wallace was 52 and Aunt Mac was 39 years old and they courted for one full calendar year.

Aunt Mac and Wallace's wedding and reception were held at the place where she worked, the Thunderbird Hotel. One of the hotel managers was fond of her and insisted he sponsor the entire event.

Aunt Mac was initially at the Colonial House, but was transferred and then promoted to head of housekeeping at the Thunderbird. Both hotels were under the same management and they knew that she was considerate of others, a leader and a good worker. Aunt Mac said, "Those good old boys sure did take to me for some old reason."

Aunt Mac enjoyed working at the Thunderbird because quite often she got the chance to bump into Nat King Cole. She said, "Around the same time I was leaving work, Nat was heading to the

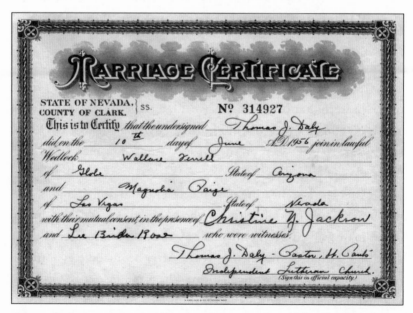

Magnolia's marriage certificate to her seventh and last husband.
Geran Family Collection

showroom. He and I spoke to each other many nights as we passed by the steamy pots and sizzling pans in the hotel's kitchen."

The maids were crazy about Nat. Before Nat King Cole even knew what his return date would be at the Thunderbird Hotel, Aunt Mac said the maids were well aware. They were in love with Nat and just knowing he was in the hotel sent throughout each and every room the smell of class and a touch of dignity.

ॐ❖ॐ

Wallace lived on the outskirts of Las Vegas near McCarran Airport. His farm consisted of hens, chickens, pigs, roosters, turkeys and horses. His small cottage sat on a hill, surrounded by twelve acres of beautiful green grass framed by a white picket fence. His neighbors included Lubertha Johnson, a lifetime NAACP

Black service workers pose in front of Thunderbird Hotel sign. Aunt Mac is in the center between two maids in black uniforms. Special Collections, UNLV Library

member and grocery store owner, and Old Man Mishey, a water well owner.

Wallace was an only child and his parents were early settlers in Las Vegas during the railroad days. When they died, he inherited the property as well as a 1929 Model A Ford.

Aunt Mac loved riding in the Model A, especially in the back. She said it was called the mother-in-law seat because they are known to be instigators. So in order for them not to hear what was being said, it was best to have them sit in the back.

Aunt Mac said she loved when Nemrod, a black man who owned a hog farm, would stop by the house and watch Wallace work on his Model A. Nemrod was known around town as a close friend of a well-known white attorney named Mike Hines. "Nemrod was to Mike like Gold Dollar was to Benny Binion," Aunt Mac said.

Friend and neighbor Carl working on Wallace's 1929 Model A Ford. Geran Family Collection

Nemrod would take care of Mike's horses at his ranch near Sahara Avenue and Jones Boulevard. Mike would host barbecues and invite all the attorneys in town. Gold Dollar brought his secret barbecue sauce that everyone loved, and of course he did all the cooking, while his wife, Lee Birda, prepared the potato salad.

Aunt Mac said Mike Hines was the nicest man anyone could meet. Segregation had no meaning for him. It was nothing for Mike to hitch a ride with a black person or defend him like he was his friend. When Mike Hines found out that Nemrod had been denied the opportunity to purchase a parcel of land in Mesquite, 80 miles northeast of Las Vegas, because he was black, he got mad and decided to get even. He told the property owner that a black guy was moving onto his land located next door. Just as Mike predicted, the owner immediately placed a "for sale" sign on his property, and the next day Nemrod bought it. Aunt Mac said that for a man who owned quite a bit of property, Nemrod seemed to get a kick out of walking around looking like a bum.

Wallace was a member of an auto club, and each year he would participate in the Old Timers Historical Parade, which was held in Yuma, Arizona. He and his friend Carl would spend all day cleaning and waxing the precious Model A, so that it would shine like a show piece.

Aunt Mac dreaded having to drive to Yuma and stay for two whole days. She said they were long days and that the farm-like little town rolled its sidewalks up at nine o'clock. What she missed most was Las Vegas' bright lights and twenty-four-hour convenience.

Wallace had a rooster he named Old Rooster. It crowed at the break of dawn. When it was still dark outside, Aunt Mac would grab a lantern and yell "Cock-a-doodle you" to the bird.

She loved singing, off-key, child-like songs while she fed the animals. Her favorite went something like this: "The rooster chews tobacco and the hen dips snuff. The old biddy can't do nothing but he sho' can strut his stuff." On the last verse she would put her hands on her hips, swing them left and right and say, "Now eat."

Wallace taught Aunt Mac a lot about farm life. She learned how to milk a cow and how to go out to the barn and kill what she wanted to prepare for dinner.

Aunt Mac's fear of becoming just a cotton picker in the fields or having to settle never came to fruition. She was now the co-owner of a farm and she had just been promoted as the head of housekeeping.

On her last trip to Mississippi, she made it a point to bring back a suitcase filled with cotton. She gathered the seeds from the cotton and had Wallace plow four rows on the side of the house,

Magnolia surrounded by friends at birthday party. Wallace stands at right, in front. Geran Family Collection

156

near her bedroom window. After each row was completed, she threw a handful of the seeds and carefully watered them.

Aunt Mac said she wanted the white hairs on the plant to be the first thing she saw in the morning when she opened her eyes. She wanted it to serve as a reminder of where she had been and how far she had come.

The most common reason she divorced her husbands was because of their excessive gambling. Wallace only gambled when friends or relatives visited from out of town. As soon as left the airport, the first thing they wanted to do was hit the casinos.

Wallace worked downtown as a chef at the El Cortez. Aunt Mac loved the fact that he was an excellent cook, because she wasn't. Fussing over a stove was the last thing she wanted to do.

Aunt Mac and Wallace didn't have kids. She said it just wasn't in her cards. Whenever she was asked this question, Aunt Mac would give the, "none of your damn business" silent treatment. Aunt Mac was a woman with no games, no make-up and no kids.

In 1995, at age 80, Aunt Mac died. It was her wish to fill the curious minds with the knowledge and wisdom contained within these pages, so that they may no longer remain in the dark.

"And for God's sake, live life to the fullest and care less about what others think."

Chapter

Last Words

For inquire I pray thee, of the former age, and
prepare thyself to the search of their fathers:
For we are but of yesterday, and know nothing,
because our days upon earth are a shadow.
Job 8:8-9

In the article published by *Ebony* magazine, "Negroes Can't Win in Las Vegas," the writer described the blacks in Las Vegas as being in lowly positions. On the contrary, Aunt Mac said the maids in the hotels were often reminded that they were the backbone of the city.

I remember asking Aunt Mac what was within her that made her stand up when the odds appeared to be solidly against her. She was a black woman from the South with little education, no family and no money, just a dream. Her response was, "Learn to say yes to what you want and leave the no for later."

Aunt Mac knew she was going to have a rough life so she simply wanted to make the best of it. She said to always know how you want your life to end, then plan from there. "All my actions, including the divorces, led me to the final chapter I envisioned in my latter years." Aunt Mac believed you must have a vision first, then action, that desires must manifest in the spiritual world first before they do so in the physical world. Never let your ego make a decision for you, she often said, because the consequences could literally ruin your life. Aunt Mac worked as a maid for many years. She said, "When you have a job, regardless what it is, you have a chance."

It seemed as though titles were insignificant for blacks in Las Vegas. A. Philip Randolph was a Pullman porter and Arthur McCants was a barber with hardly any education. Gold Dollar was a man who knew how to sign his name but seldom did anyone see him read or write, except for a few sections of the newspaper. He saved Benny Binion's life, a white man who never forgot it. While growing up, Binion was referred to as illiterate. So how did he become one of the most powerful and richest men in Las Vegas history? Binion had so much money, he was able to display a million in a plastic case in his casino so tourists could take pictures in front of it.

These men were not sold on the idea that a title is what allowed you to have a voice in society. What they felt you must have, however, was a committed passion and desire to unravel the cloth society hands you so that you can create your own blanket of comfort.

In order to lift the veil of prejudice, it was crucial for the blacks in Las Vegas to challenge the laws and then test them. They discovered that behind the veil was the face of truth, and that face had many colors. The greatest legacy the black residents and entertainers in Las Vegas leave is not so much what was accomplished, but how they helped others to accomplish. They are truly American pioneering heroes and their selfless sacrifices and stubbornness made their dream of making a decent living in a decent city come true.

Bibliography

Books and Articles

Albert, Peter J., and Ronald Hoffman. *We Shall Overcome – Martin Luther King, Jr. and the Black Freedom Struggle*. New York: Da Capo Press, 1993.

Bailey, Pearl. *The Raw Pearl*. New York: Pocket Books, 1973.

Berman, Susan. *Lady Las Vegas*. New York: A&E Network Books, Inc., 1996.

Carpozi, George. *Bugsy*. New York: Pinnacle Books, 1973.

Collier, James Lincoln. *Louis Armstrong: An American Genius*. New York: Oxford University Press, 1983.

Cole, Marie. *An Intimate Biography*. New York: William Morrow and Company, 1971.

Current, Richard N., T. Harry Williams and Frank Freidel. *American History: A Survey*. New York: Alfred A. Knopf, 1964.

Davis, Daniel S. *Mr. Black Labor*, New York: E. P. Dutton and Company, 1972. p. 104.

Davis, Sammy, Jr., with Jane and Burt Boyar. *Why Me? The Sammy Davis, Jr. Story*. New York: Farrar, Straus and Giroux, 1989.

Foner, Philip S. *W.E.B Du Bois Speaks*. New York: Pathfinder, 1970.

Franklin, John Hope. *From Slavery to Freedom*. New York: Alfred A. Knopf, 1980.

Freedman, Leonard. *Public Housing: The Politics of Poverty*. New York: Holt, Rinehart and Winston, 1969.

Goodrich, James. *Negroes Can't Win in Las Vegas. Ebony* magazine, March Issue. Chicago: Johnson Publishing Company. 1954.

Horne, Lena, and Richard Schickel. *Lena*. New York: Doubleday, 1965.

Kitt, Eartha. *Thursday's Child*. New York: Van Rees Press, 1956. p. 243-44.

Kleinsorge, Paul L. *The Boulder Canyon Project*, Stanford: Stanford University Press, 1941. p. 301.

Knepp, Donn. *Las Vegas – The Entertainment Capital of the World*. California: Lane Publishing Co., 1987.

Land, Barbara, and Myrick Land. *A Short History of Las Vegas*. Nevada: University of Nevada Press, Reno, 1999. p. 60, 96.

Lewis, Georgia. *The Way It Was: Diary of A Pioneer Las Vegas Woman*. Las Vegas: Sun Publishing Company, 1979.

Medelson, Wallace. *Discrimination*. New Jersey: Prentice Hall, 1962.

Shaw, Arnold. *Belafonte: An Unauthorized Biography*. Philadelphia: Chilton Company, 1980.

Osofsky, Gilbert. *Harlem: The Making of a Ghetto*. New York: Harper Torchbooks, 1963.

Paher, Stanley. *Las Vegas: As It Began, As It Grew*. Las Vegas: Nevada Publications, 1971.

Perry, John. *Washington and George Washington Carver, Unshakable Faith*. Oregon: Multnomah Publishers, 1999.

Reid, Ed, and Ovid Demaris. *The Green Felt Jungle*, New York: Buccaneer Books, Incorporated, 1963.

Rose, Harold M. *The Black Ghetto*. New York: McGraw Hill, 1971.

Washington, Booker T. *Up From Slavery*, New York: The Heritage Press, 1970, p. 15.

Wilkerson III, W. R. *The Man Who Invented Las Vegas*, Beverly Hills: Ciro's Books, 2000.

Newspapers

Las Vegas Age:
  Colored Voters. April 26, 1935.
  Colored Section. March 15, 1932.
  First Blacks Hired On Dam. July 8, 1932.
  Nigger Hill Made Real Mining History. August 17, 1933, p.1.
  Darky Prospectors Answers Call of Spirit World. October 6, 1933, p.1.
  Dam Completed. September 27, 1935.
  Coon Songs. February 6, 1926.
  President Dedicates Dam. September 23, 1935.
  Two Florida Darkies. July 9, 1921.
  Two Hundred Prominent Colored People. October 30,1928.
  Zion Rest Mission. January 6, 1917.
  Cartoon With Black Mammy Figure. January 18, 1930.

Las Vegas Review-Journal:
  Blacks in Bouls Town. December 28, 1934.
  Envoy Here to Aid Negroes In Getting Work. November 19, 1933.
  Fred Hesse Elected. May 8, 1925.
  Growth and Economic Development. January 1, 1930.
  Klan Parade. November 14, 1924.
  Las Vegas' Black Pioneers. June 4, 1972.
  Race and Color Bill. February 15, 1939.
  Vagrancy Laws. April 5, 1932.
  White Prostitutes Better than Negro. March 26, 1932.

Las Vegas Sun:
  Obituary of Louis "Louie" Wiener, Jr. Ed Koch and Bill Gang February 7, 1996.
  Vegas Color Barrier Lifted After Parley & Businesses In Vegas Lift Color Barrier.
  March 26, 1960. Front Page (two versions printed).
  Where We Stand – Hank talks about Arthur McCants. March 26, 1960.

Census Records

Historical Statistics of the United States: Colonial Times to 1970, U.S. Department of Commerce.

Sixteenth Census of the United States, 1940. U.S. Department of Commerce, Washington, D.C.: U.S. Printing Office, 1940.

Thirteenth Census of the United States, 1910. U.S. Department of Commerce. Washington, D.C.: U.S. Printing Office, 1910. Vol. 2.

Oral Histories

Cahlan, John T. *Reminisces of a Reno and Las Vegas, Nevada, Newspaperman, University Regent, and Public-Spirited Citizen.* Interview by Mary Ellen Glass, 1968. University of Nevada Oral History Project. Special Collections, University of Nevada, Reno, Library.

Elliott, Gary T., and R.T. King. *Fighting Back.* Interview with James B. McMillan, 1997. University of Nevada Oral History Project. Reference Section, West Las Vegas Library.

Fitzgerald, Roosevelt. *The Evolution of a Black Community in Las Vegas 1905-1940.* Oral History Project. Special Collections, University of Nevada, Las Vegas, Lied Library.

Personal Interviews

Eugene "Peve" Buford,
Magnolia Ferrell
Roosevelt Fitzgerald
Hazel Geran
George Jacobs
Ed Koch
Lee Birda Rose
Calvin "Eagle Eye" Shields
Erwin "Brother" Wilburn

Photo Credits

Buford Family Collection (Private Collection)

Donald Clark and Lloyd Gill (Private Collection)

Geran Family Collection (Private Collection)

Oakland Library, African American References, Sections: Athletes, Musicians, Movie Stars

Rose Family Collection (Private Collection)

University of Nevada Las Vegas, Special Collections: Afro-Americans in Las Vegas

West Las Vegas Library.

Document Credits

Roosevelt Fitzgerald: Handwritten letter from R.J. Christensen to County Commissioners

Petition submitted by Arthur McCants, A. M. Brantford of the NAACP, and the Zion Mission Sunday School to Mayor and Alderman of the City of Las Vegas.

Index

Town Tavern, New, 111, 113, 135, 136
Treniers, The, 109, 113, 116, 121
Turman, Earl, 111

U

Uncle Jake's Barbeque, 30
United Services Organization (USO), 60

V

Vagrancy law, 45
Van Skee, Father, 38
Venus Room, 132
Victory Village, 56

W

Walker, Mr., 119
Walker, Prentiss, 32
Wallace. *See* Ferrel, Wallace
Wallace, P. W., 38
War Memorial Building, 108
West, Dr. Charles, 140
Westside, 23, 25, 26, 27, 28, 29, 37, 38, 40, 41, 47, 48, 49, 55, 57, 59, 60, 61, 62, 66, 67, 68, 69, 72, 76, 79, 81, 84, 93, 95, 96, 98, 104, 105, 110, 111, 114, 120, 121, 128, 135, 136, 138, 143, 149
Westside Improvement Association, 47
Whipple, Reed, 143
White, Slappy, 115, 116
Wiener, Louis Jr., 100
Wilkerson, W. R. "Billy", 89, 90, 91, 100, 102

Will Mastin Trio, 103, 104, 108, 129
World War II, 50, 52, 57, 59, 62

Z

Zion Mission, 34, 38
Zion Rest Mission Sunday School, 38